A PRACTICAL GUIDE
ENJOYABLE PRAYE

MW00824417

HARP
—&—
BOWL
HANDBOOK

MIKE BICKLE

FORERUNNER
PUBLISHING

KANSAS CITY, MISSOURI

Harp and Bowl Handbook: A Practical Guide to Sustaining Enjoyable Prayer Meetings
by Mike Bickle

Published by Forerunner Publishing
International House of Prayer
3535 E. Red Bridge Road
Kansas City, Missouri 64137
ihopkc.org/books

Forerunner Publishing is the book-publishing division of the International House of Prayer of Kansas City, an evangelical missions organization that exists to partner in the Great Commission by advancing 24/7 prayer and proclaiming the beauty of Jesus and His glorious return.

ISBN: 978-1-938060-42-7
eBook ISBN: 978-1-938060-43-4

Cover design by Joshua Fenimore, George Estrada
Interior design by Dale Jimmo

Printed in the United States of America

28 27 26 25 24 23 22 21 20   1 2 3 4 5 6 7 8 9

CONTENTS

4. Enjoyable Prayer—Sixteen Values of the Harp and Bowl Model | 43

5. What We Do in Our Prayer Room | 55

6. Jesus, the Bridegroom King | 59

7. The End-Time Prayer Movement | 61

8. The Levites—The Full-Time Occupation of Singers and Musicians | 65

9. The Call to Be a Full-Time Intercessory Missionary | 71

10. Prayer Outlines | 85

1

Prayer in the Spirit of the Tabernacle of David

The Holy Spirit is orchestrating a global prayer and worship movement in these days. It will far surpass any other prayer movement in church history. The Holy Spirit is equipping the Church to partner with Jesus' intercessory prayer ministry at the right hand of the Father. The end result is the great harvest of new believers being added to the kingdom of God. The number of people coming to Jesus at the present hour across the nations is unprecedented in history. I believe this will continue to increase numerically. Jesus will not return to a prayerless Church, but to one enjoying mature partnership with Him in intercession for the great harvest. The gospel of the kingdom will be preached to all nations before Jesus returns (Mt. 24:14).

A New Name

"'My house shall be called a house of prayer for all nations'" (Isa. 56:7). The prophet Isaiah had much to say about the end-time global prayer and worship movement. He described a time when God's people worldwide would experience unusual grace and authority in prayer, emphasizing this by declaring that God would call His Church a *house of prayer*. This prophetic naming is, in itself, a promise of the Church being empowered by God's grace to pray in a powerful way. All over the earth, it will become common to hear of prayer ministries being sustained for many hours each week and of ministries teaming up together to offer 24/7 prayer (24 hours a day, 7 days a week) in their region, as many churches work together in their city or region.

Enjoyable Prayer

Isaiah also prophesied a totally new paradigm of prayer that would be characterized by *joy*. The Lord promised, "'I will ... make them *joyful* in My house of prayer'" (Isa. 56:7). In other words, the Holy Spirit will lead the Church in a way that believers will experience *"enjoyable prayer"*—prayer that is refreshing and invigorating. If prayer is not enjoyable, it will not happen in a sustained way. Historically, prayer has been hard—and thus greatly neglected. Yet new days of refreshing, enjoyable prayer are breaking forth even now. Imagine the implications of enjoyable prayer. The climate within the Body of Christ worldwide will be different because of deep partnership in prayer with Jesus, the eternal intercessor and our Bridegroom King.

The Spirit of the Tabernacle of David

I believe the end-time global prayer movement will operate in the spirit of the tabernacle of David. What was the tabernacle of David? What will it look like in the future? I do not claim to have complete answers to these oft-asked questions, though it speaks of the restoration of the throne of David, including David's worship ministry. In Jerusalem, King David built a special tent, called a *tabernacle*, to house the ark of the covenant (1 Chr. 15:1; 16:1). David assigned musicians and singers to minister before the ark. He organized *4,000 musicians* and *288 singers* to minister to God in shifts that continued day and night (1 Chr. 6:31–32; 15:16–22; 23:4–6). David provided financially for them, releasing them to worship as their *full-time occupation* (1 Chr. 9:33; 25:7). As full-time ministers, they had the opportunity to develop and excel (1 Chr. 25:1–7; 2 Chr. 29:27).

The Heavenly Symphony and the Beauty of God

In Revelation 4–5, John described the heavenly symphony that continues non-stop before God's throne. The ideal model of worship is seen in those who worship before God's throne (Rev. 4–5). Jesus taught us to pray that God's will be done "on earth as it is in heaven" (Mt. 6:10). Revelation 4–5 gives insight on how to *worship* God on earth *as He is worshiped in heaven*.

No other passage of Scripture gives more insight into the beauty that surrounds God's throne. The jasper, sardius, and emerald glory is only a hint of the splendor of God's beauty being displayed. I sometimes speak of this as the "beauty realm of God." Oh, to live fascinated with God's beauty! Those nearest Him are filled with marvel, awe, and wonder. Touching this reality in even a small way is to live exhilarated with God. Oh, to live on earth as awestruck worshipers of God!

Feasting on the beauty of God was foundational to the way David worshiped God. The primary desire of his life was to behold God's beauty (Ps. 27:4; 145:5). The *beauty realm of God* is foundational to intercessory worship in the spirit of the tabernacle of David. As we feast on God's beauty, our heart becomes fascinated.

Harp and Bowl Intercessory Worship

The heavenly elders and the four living creatures came to Jesus with two things—*a harp* and *a bowl*.

> *[8] Now when He had taken the scroll, the four living creatures and the twenty-four elders fell down before the Lamb, each having a harp, and golden bowls full of incense, which are the prayers of the saints. (Rev. 5:8)*

The *harp* speaks of God's music (and worship songs); the *bowl* speaks of prayer. In other words, the worship around the throne incorporates prayer together with music and songs. One key to the "enjoyable prayer" about which Isaiah prophesied (Isa. 56:7) is to engage in prayer *in the context of* worship with prophetic music and singers. When the harp (worship music) comes together with the bowl (intercession), prayer is enjoyable.

God ordained that the worship music around the throne flow in an interactive way with prayers that are offered. In the book of Revelation, worship often flows with prayer in what I refer to as intercessory worship. The spirit of worship gives wings to prayer. We call this the *harp and bowl model of intercessory worship*. I believe it is integral to the present worldwide prayer movement. Many churches are beginning new prayer initiatives, and many houses of prayer are being started—these prayer rooms will be fueled by songs of love and adoration to Jesus. As worship songs are joined with intercession for the nations, great spiritual benefits are released on earth.

We are seeking to learn how worship music can flow with intercession in an interactive way. Intercessory prayer joined with anointed music unlocks a unique part of our heart. Moreover, it helps to unify intercessors.

We read that, in his tabernacle, King David valued the prophetic spirit resting on the singers and musicians (1 Chr. 25:1–3). So also in our prayer meetings, it is important to learn how the prophetic spirit can flow more freely on the musicians, singers, and intercessors in an interactive way. David also emphasized responsive, or antiphonal, singers and choirs that sang and answered one another in song (Ezra 3:11; Neh. 12:24).

The Restoration of the Tabernacle of David

At the Jerusalem council, the apostle James confronted a crisis related to the Gentiles coming into the kingdom of God. In the midst of this, James quoted a prophecy from Amos 9:11 about God's promise to rebuild the tabernacle of David (Acts 15:14–18). Although James' primary point here concerned the Gentiles being saved by faith, a secondary point can be seen related to God's glory being restored to Israel, including the reality of David's order of worship—thus, *worship in the spirit of the tabernacle of David.*

> ¹⁶"*I ... will rebuild the tabernacle of David, which has fallen down ... ¹⁷ so that the rest of mankind may seek the L*ORD, *even all the Gentiles ...*'" (Acts 15:16–17)

God has chosen to restore the spirit of the tabernacle of David as one essential element in releasing the fullness of prayer unto revival in the nations. The intercessory worship ministry of the tabernacle of David will be restored in a way that is related to the Great Commission and will include the gospel being preached in every nation (Mt. 24:14) including Israel and to the Jewish people. We can be assured of success, knowing that there will be believers from every tribe, tongue, and nation standing before God on the last day (Rev. 5:9; 7: 9–10; 14:6; 15:4).

An Historical Example of Prayer Affecting Missions

In 1727, a young, wealthy German nobleman, Count Zinzendorf, committed his Herrnhut estate in what used to be East Germany to a 24/7 prayer ministry (*Herrnhut* means "watch of the Lord"). This Moravian prayer ministry continued 24 hours a day for over 100 years. The nobleman who led this 24/7 prayer furnace also led the first Protestant missionary movement in history. He sent out the intercessors, two by two, to unreached people groups in the earth. As they were sent out in evangelism, the prayer furnace at Herrnhut covered them, interceded for them. In other words, the first Protestant missionary movement flowed out from 24/7 prayer joined with preaching, resulting in the advancing of the Great Commission.

Our Story in Kansas City

In May 1983, our church hosted twenty-one days of prayer with fasting for revival. During this time, the Lord spoke to us saying that He would establish in our midst a *24/7 prayer ministry in the spirit of the tabernacle of David.*

Of course, we did not understand what this meant. Our first response was to seek to be faithful in the small beginnings of a prayer ministry in our church. The Lord graciously helped us to establish an intercessory ministry that continued for five to six hours each day for most of the next sixteen years, before the International House of Prayer of Kansas City began on May 7, 1999. In other words, for sixteen years (1983–1999), we continued in daily prayer meetings while waiting for the Lord to release us into a 24/7 prayer and worship schedule.

On May 7, 1999, we began in a 300-seat building about one mile from our church. We began with thirteen hours a day of intercession, led by worship teams. Then, four months later, on September 19, we expanded to the full 24-hour schedule, seven days a week. By the grace of God, we are continuing to this day.

2

WHY THE HARP AND BOWL MODEL?

I. What We Mean by Our Harp and Bowl Model

A. When we refer to our "Harp and Bowl" model, the *harp* speaks of worshiping God with musical instruments, and the *bowl* speaks of the prayers of the Church.

> *8 The twenty-four elders ... each having a harp, and golden bowls full of incense, which are the prayers of the saints. (Rev. 5:8)*

B. There are many ways to express this model. Every ministry and house of prayer will have a different expression that will develop over time. Our ministry in Kansas City is just one of the many valid expressions of combining worship and prayer.

II. Experiencing a Greater Flow of the Holy Spirit

A. If people in our midst understand the whys (the values) behind the whats (the mechanics) then they more easily embrace our Harp and Bowl prayer model. Loyalty to a model without understanding the underlying heart values that shape it leads to frustrating formalism. We must understand the values behind the principles.

B. Our desire is to discern the structure that enhances the flow of the Holy Spirit. The Harp and Bowl model is designed on the premise that a right structure enhances a creative expression of the Holy Spirit in the context of a corporate team even more than individualistic spontaneous expression.

C. Within a symphony, there are governing principles that give it organization and form and are conducive to allowing a corporate, complex, multifaceted and diverse, yet unified and harmonious, creative expression to be realized.

D. Without these principles, the form of "symphony" could not exist. The governing principles facilitate rather than hinder the creative expression of the corporate whole.

E. One priority is to empower hearts with confidence that overcomes fear.

III. Our Quest and Passion for Fullness of the Spirit

A. Paul taught us that only together <u>with all the saints</u> can we experience the ocean of God's love. The fullness is only released to the unified Church.

> *[18] ... may be able to comprehend <u>with all the saints</u> what is the width and length and depth and height— [19] to know the love of Christ ... that you may be <u>filled with all the fullness of God</u>. (Eph. 3:18–19)*

B. The longing for fullness of God's promises is a foundational heart cry at IHOPKC. It is the reason we persevere through some of the challenging seasons of ministry.

IV. The Value of Unified Prayer—The Context for Fullness

A. *Commanded Blessing*

> *[1] Behold, how good and how pleasant it is for brethren <u>to dwell together in unity</u>! ... [3] <u>for there</u> the LORD commanded the blessing—life forevermore. (Ps. 133:1, 3)*

1. This speaks of the manifestation of the Spirit's power in a way that neither men nor devils can stop. I believe that in the generation the Lord returns, the miracles seen in the book of Exodus and the book of Acts will be combined and multiplied on a global scale. The commanded blessing points to the greatest demonstration of power that is available to the church today.

> *[12] "... he who believes in Me, the works that I do he will do also; and <u>greater works than these he will do</u>, because I go to My Father." (Jn. 14:12)*

2. Our vision for the International House of Prayer of Kansas City is to enter into the "commanded blessing" of the Lord. Some are not aware of the divine possibilities available only in unified anointed prayer. There is a ceiling in the spirit until the prayer flows in unity in the Spirit (2 Cor. 1:11).

B. Praying in unity was vital to the release of the Spirit on the day of Pentecost.

> *[14] These all continued with <u>one accord in prayer and supplication</u>. (Acts 1:14)*

> *[1] ... they were <u>all with one accord in one place</u>. [2] And suddenly there came a sound from heaven, as of a <u>rushing mighty wind, and it filled the whole house</u> ... (Acts 2:1–2)*

> *[12] And through the hands of the apostles <u>many signs and wonders</u> were done among the people. And they were <u>all with one accord</u> in Solomon's Porch. (Acts 5:12)*

V. Three Values that Facilitate Unity in Prayer

A. ***Value #1: Mature Team Ministry***—we go further together as a symphony

1. Team ministry is necessary: 1) between the worship team and the intercessor; 2) between the worship leader and prophetic singers as they sing antiphonally; 3) among all in the prayer room.

2. The unified symphony is the goal because fullness only comes as we function in this way. God has put a limitation on each of us so that we can't have a symphony without each other. The Holy Spirit gives more as we function together in unity (1 Cor. 12–14).

3. Necessary elements of a symphony:

   a. Skilled hands—practicing for years on our instruments

   b. Trained minds—learning much about the music

   c. Unified teams—flowing together as a team may be more difficult for some great musicians. To play with necessary musical restraints to bring out the best of the team

4. The conductor of the symphony must have the ability to manage the ego of the musical stars.

5. An analogy of a championship basketball team—ability to manage the ego of the stars is an important role of a head coach. We are more committed to the team being great than to a few gifted individuals showcasing their superior abilities.

6. Being on a unified team will bring the best out of all on the team.

B. **Value #2: Inclusiveness**—everyone can participate

1. In light of our global mandate, we must have a model that the less gifted can function in on a regular basis. Team ministry allows for the immediate inclusion those who are beginners on their team. Malachi 4:6 teaches us that the old and young must flow together, mature and immature, seasoned and unseasoned musically.

2. Our goal is to convince the less gifted ones that they are wanted and belong on the team. We must have a model that can reach many in the nations, not just the musically elite.

C. **Value #3: Centrality of the Word**—unifies our hearts with His and others'

1. One missing element in much of the prayer and worship movement today is the Scripture itself. IHOPKC is called by God to be a "singing seminary," not just a gathering of church musicians who love music yet do not seek to gain depth in the Word. We rejoice in the language of God's heart without being frustrated by the limitation of biblical language. Singing and praying the Word results in a discipleship program—a "singing seminary."

2. Using the Scriptures in prayer and worship hinders error and weirdness.

VI. Cultivating Confidence

A. Our paradigm of how the Spirit moves—the Lord makes Himself easy to find and to partner with (the God of the "big target"). Jesus is a far greater teacher and leader than we are students and followers. The God of great patience is not an insecure dove who easily gets offended and driven away. Yes, the Spirit can be grieved, but even in that He draws back to awaken more hunger in us.

B. Demystifying the process—the model must demystify the spiritual dynamics in order to be inclusive. To value inclusiveness is to help undermine spiritual/mystical pride. We sought to create a model that can work even when people are tired and feeling a bit dull.

C. Confidence is an essential element in flowing in the Spirit. Our model acts as a permission-giving mechanism to dismantle fear. The model gives permission. It empowers and gives boldness. Seeking to flow spontaneously and prophetically in front of others can be stressful and difficult. However, when the responsibility for doing something new is placed on the model, it removes the fear and empowers people.

D. Confidence and boldness in God are important to develop in order to equip people to flow in the anointing of the Spirit. One hindrance to flowing in the anointing of the Spirit is fear or timidity.

E. Our prayer model is based on values that seek to dismantle fear in our intercessors, prophetic singers and musicians, etc. Only as our fears begin to be subdued can we soar together as a team. Fear locks our hearts. We must dismantle our fears in order to flow with creativity in God.

F. The discomfort of being out of our comfort zone is not the same as quenching the Spirit. It is awkward to flow at an intimate heart level with people we don't know very well and when we lack clearly defined expectations of what we are to do in the team.

G. There are necessary human dynamics involved in operating in the anointing of the Spirit. These dynamics must be easy to understand so we are not preoccupied with the human mechanics. In this way, they become second nature to us so that in time we can become fully preoccupied with God Himself as we flow in the Holy Spirit in our model.

H. Learning to flow together in the emotional and spiritual dynamics of prophetic worship can be a struggle because it is naturally awkward. This natural and inevitable struggle is sometimes wrongly misinterpreted as a spiritual hindrance. In other words, people think the Spirit isn't moving or that they can't flow freely in the Spirit when in reality there are usually just awkward human dynamics.

I. There are common fears that must be overcome as we cultivate confidence.

   1. The fear of the unfamiliar: the fear of not knowing the model or the Bible, or simply the fear of being wrong, commonly hinder confidence.

   2. The fear of missing God: many have a fear of quenching the Holy Spirit. In other words, they fear failing God or being disqualified spiritually.

3. The fear of rejection: we serve with people who have different personalities, abilities, perspectives of God, and expectations. This can lead to a fear of being rejected by them.

4. The fear of not being wanted: many have a fear of not being good enough to be on the team.

5. The fear of being hurt: some fear being criticized and judged by leaders or team members.

6. The fear of failure (shame): the fear of failing in front of others is a major struggle. The fear of performing poorly in our skills and abilities hinders us. It is awkward to flow at an intimate heart level with God in front of some who we perceive can do it better than us.

7. The fear of being replaced: this can lead to comparison and competition.

VII. Structure That Facilitates Creativity and Spontaneity

A. We value structure that facilitates spontaneity. Our structure is a permission-giving mechanism and communication tool that leads to greater spontaneity or flow in the Spirit. An effective structure helps people to flow together in unity as a team in the Spirit.

B. Our goal is to provide opportunity for Spirit-inspired creativity that includes familiar corporate worship songs and spontaneous new songs and expressions of music.

C. Our model is primarily a communication tool that enables our singers, musicians, and prayer leader to flow together with confidence and without timidity or hesitation.

D. The structure identifies the times and ways when various members of the team have liberty to be more creative with their instrument or voice. This makes prayer more enjoyable. It is vital in maintaining a 24/7 schedule.

E. Clearly defined roles and expectations lead to greater confidence and unity for the members of a worship team to express themselves in ways agreed upon as set forth in our model. Our structure identifies the places where our singers and musicians have options to be creative.

F. *Sustainable flow:* We can be more creative with structure. We can launch out in spontaneity, then land back within the structure to get ready to launch again.

G. *All music styles are encouraged:* Our model is a communication tool that can be expressed within various musical styles. We do not ask our worship teams to use only one or two music styles; rather, we encourage many different styles.

H. *Transferable within all our IHOPKC worship teams:* Singers and musicians can easily switch between teams (for example, one singer filling in for another singer who is sick), because we all use the same model and terminology. Therefore, when we periodically improve our model across the 24/7 spectrum, all changes to our model are established through our Global Prayer Room (GPR) section leaders, with strong input from the worship leaders, and then presented to all of our singers and musicians.

VIII.   Why We Ask Worship Leaders to Lead With an Instrument

A. ***Premise:*** One strong value that our leadership team has held since 1999 is that our worship leaders lead using their instruments. There are several reasons that we emphasize this value. Here are some of the reasons given by IHOPKC worship leaders over the years.

B. ***Modeling:*** Part of our assignment from the Lord is to model and equip young worship leaders to lead in prayer rooms. Since 1999, we have impacted many young worship leaders who lead in prayer rooms around the world. Our target is to model how to lead worship in a prayer room, rather than how to lead a worship concert. Worship concerts are good, but they have a different function than leading a prayer room. A person with a charismatic personality and a good voice may be able to lead a worship concert without being proficient on an instrument. Why? They can use the same songs as they travel—it is common for one's worship concerts to closely resemble each other. "Choreographed creativity" works well for worship concerts and traveling teams—but leading twelve hours a week in a prayer room requires much more diversity and creativity. A worship team must develop musical proficiency to have the creativity necessary to lead many worship sets a week in the same prayer room, year after year.

C. ***Creativity:*** Worship leaders who are proficient on their instrument can go many more places musically and are, therefore, able to lead their band into greater musical creativity.

D. **Leadership:** Worship leaders need to be able to *lead* their team with their instrument as well as their voice. Worship leaders need to lead the music—whoever directs the instruments is the one leading the room. Leading the music enables them to develop musically in leading their worship team; meaning, they will be able to flow together regardless of who is playing on their worship team (since we have fill-ins and turnover of our musicians). When traveling to lead worship at a conference, often a worship leader may not be able to bring a team but will need to use a local team. Worship leaders who excel in leading from their instrument will be better equipped to lead with strength in these situations. When worship leaders travel to a minister at a conference (without their team), they will be able to lead the local musicians, with whom they have not practiced, with more skill and liberty if they (the worship leaders) are proficient in leading on their instrument.

E. **Skill development:** It is important that worship leaders *grow* in their musicality. Playing an instrument throughout a two-hour set, six times per week, gives opportunities for them to cultivate excellence, proficiency, and confidence on their instrument and in leading their band.

F. **Longevity:** Worship leaders who are proficient with their instruments usually have greater *longevity* as an artist. Often those who have only developed their voice rather than proficiency on a musical instrument do not have the same longevity in leading worship over decades.

G. **Songwriting:** Those proficient on their instrument are usually more creative in songwriting.

H. **Stability:** We agree that a worship leader can lead a prayer meeting without using their instrument, but the issue is, can they lead six prayer meetings a week for years? Teams turn over regularly in the house of prayer movement for various reasons, so a worship leader may have a great team for a season and then may have less experienced musicians in the following season. In contrast, a well-known traveling worship leader has the finances to pay a band for years.

I.   ***Conclusion:*** The value of leading with an instrument has significant implications on the landscape of the prayer movement. If our worship leaders do not lead with their instrument, then the young worship leaders from IHOPKC's Forerunner Music Academy will not want to "bother" leading with an instrument—then worship leaders in houses of prayer (that follow us) will do the same. After a few years, the musicality of our movement will be lower. Therefore, we insist that our worship leaders lead using their instrument—we ask them to play it during the *majority* of their two-hour worship sets.

J.   ***Thoughts from a few of our worship leaders:***

"We do a severe injustice to our young worship leaders by not compelling them to learn an instrument well. They need thousands of hours of reps to become skillful on their instruments, and thus to lead better when the glory hits in a greater way, not leaning so much on programmed sounds (synthesizers and electronic equipment). Creativity comes from mastering their instrument from many hours of reps. This is essential even if your voice is your main instrument—it will be enhanced by excellent musicality." **Rachel Faagutu**

"Often the longevity of a worship leader's ministry is connected to their ability to play an instrument well. They will write more songs instead of mostly sing cover songs. We encourage worship leaders to be songwriters. A worship leader with strong musical ability will be able to use a local band when traveling instead of being at their 'mercy.' We have people with very strong voices, but they do not get invited to lead worship in our places because they do not lead the band in their worship team." **Misty Edwards**

"Some young people who are new at leading worship do not want to lead with an instrument because they are not yet proficient on their instrument. They watch famous worship leaders online lead without an instrument, and they want to be like them, so they skip learning an instrument. This sets them back as a worship leader." **Juliana Thompson**

"IHOPKC needs to uphold the value of live music in a culture where it is dying out and being replaced by electronic equipment—this is part of our prophetic impact to call the Church back to live music instead of the secular move away from it." **Chris Tofilon**

3

THE HARP AND BOWL STRUCTURE—MECHANICS AND PRINCIPLES

I. Our Four Prayer Formats

A. We use the term "prayer formats" to speak of the various expressions of our prayer model.

B. *Intercessory Prayer Format*
This prayer format focuses on praying for a breakthrough of God's justice and revival—for a dramatic outpouring of the Spirit on the Church, the lost, and on His people who serve in the various spheres of society in our city and in the nations.

C. *Worship with the Word Format*
This format provides a way to grow in our understanding of God's Word as we sing through a passage of Scripture.

D. *Prophetic Worship Format*
In this format, we focus on worshiping God, expressing our adoration and commitment to Him as the worship is inspired by the Holy Spirit.

E. *Devotional Worship Format*
This is designed to provide an anointed context in which people can sit at the feet of Jesus and meditate on the Word as they linger in God's presence.

II. Key Components of Our Prayer Model

A. *Scripture*

The foundation of all expressions of corporate worship must be Scripture.

B. *Team Ministry*

Our model is a *communication tool* to facilitate confident and inclusive team flow—singers know when they can sing spontaneously and when it is time to create a short chorus for everyone to join with, etc., while the worship band knows when they can do more spontaneous and creative music.

C. *Antiphonal Singing*

Teams go further in ministry together with responsive singing and praying.

D. *Prophetic Oracles*

The team makes room for singers to sing individual prophetic songs. A singer puts a fist on their Bible or on their palm during spontaneous singing to indicate they want to sing a prophetic oracle, then they wait until the worship leader gives them a signal to sing it. These should be sung in a declarative tone. An oracle may continue for 1–2 minutes, ending with a spontaneous chorus or a name of God to signal to the worship team that they are done. We encourage the prayer leader to isolate a phrase and the singers to develop the prophetic oracle with antiphonal singing.

E. *Spontaneous Choruses*

The lead singer (chorus leader) sings spontaneous choruses with which all join. Spontaneous choruses give opportunity for all in the room to sing the same prayer in unity.

F. *Double choruses*

The worship leader or chorus leader may occasionally establish double choruses, in which two different but complementary choruses echo back and forth, answering each other. The chorus leader or worship leader ends the double chorus even if another singer began it. In preparing for double choruses, the worship leader should designate the singer responsible to start a double chorus and which singers sing the double chorus. Worship leaders should seek to assign equal vocal strength to each group, so that both the choruses are carried with equal strength.

G. *Spontaneous Singing*

The worship leader initiates a time of spontaneous singing, including singing in the spirit or singing with our understanding by making melody in our heart as we sing the Scripture (Eph. 5:19; Col. 3:16).

H. *Musical Selahs*

Musical *selahs*, or creative spontaneous musical expressions, may continue for 5–10 minutes or longer. David trained musicians to prophesy with instruments (1 Chr. 25:1).

I. *Prayer for the Sick*

The prayer leader has the option to make room for a short time of ministry to those who want prayer for physical healing. The prayer leader prays on the microphone for the sick, while those in the room may gather around those who indicate they would like prayer for healing.

1. Healing prayer may occur at the end of any worship cycle as the worship team is preparing to go back into another worship song while others pray for the sick.

2. Suggested language to facilitate healing prayer: *If you are sick in your body and would like prayer, please raise your hand. We invite the room to be the ministry team, so let's have 2 to 3 gather around each one, stand in front of them, and pray for them.*

J. *Small-Group Prayer*

During Intercessory Prayer formats, the prayer leader may initiate a time to gather in small groups of 4 to 5 people to pray. Small-group prayer usually happens after three intercessory prayers in a worship cycle.

1. The prayer leader clarifies that participation is optional. The prayer leader does not *tell* people to participate but simply *invites* those who want to.

2. Suggested language for calling small-group prayer: *As we go into another worship song, we invite any who want to participate in small-group prayer to stand up, gather in groups of 4 to 5, and pray for any burden on your heart.*

3. The worship team should go right into a song following the invitation to small-group or healing prayer in order to facilitate participation for those not praying or being prayed for. We request that the worship leader sing an actual worship song at this time instead of a musical selah to minimize conversations among those not praying in a small group.

K.   *Rapid-Fire Prayer*

During intercessory prayer, the prayer leader may invite intercessors to come up to pray on the microphone for a specific prayer topic. We call this "rapid-fire prayer," because people pray one after another in quick succession. Shorter prayers help create room for more to participate. It incorporates 10- to 15-second prayers. The theme may cover topics like the government, nations, healing, evangelistic outreaches, university campuses, pro-life themes, etc.

1.   Suggested language for calling rapid-fire prayer: *I invite anyone to line up behind me to pray 10- to 15-second prayers for* _____ .

2.   The prayer leader begins by praying a brief prayer around the theme, then offers the microphone to the next person in line, and so on.

3.   The chorus leader will sing a spontaneous chorus after every 4–5 intercessors. The purpose of the intermittent choruses between intercessors is to help facilitate room participation.

III.   Four Elements of a Worship Cycle—Overview

A.   Each 2-hour worship set typically involves 3–5 worship cycles, which incorporate four elements:

1.   **Element #1:** Corporate worship songs

2.   **Element #2:** Spontaneous singing

3.   **Element #3:** Developing a biblical passage by antiphonal singing (four parts)
Part 1: Sing or pray through a passage of Scripture (or a biblical prayer)
Part 2: Isolate a phrase
Part 3: Develop the phrase through antiphonal singing
Part 4: Spontaneous choruses

4.   **Element #4:** Optional prayer—rapid fire, small group, for the sick, warring in the spirit

B.   Note: Our primary governing principle is to *develop a biblical passage by antiphonal singing.*

IV.   **Four Elements of a Worship Cycle—Practical Principles**

A.   *Element #1: Corporate Worship*

1.   We ask each worship leader to begin their set with a known worship song as soon as they transition. We want the room to sing, thus we ask our worship leaders to implement the following guidelines.

2.   **Songs directed to God:** As a rule, we choose songs that are sung *to* God, not just *about* Him. One *premier assignment* from the Lord in this movement is to call people to encounter the beauty of Jesus, to seek to walk out the First Commandment, and to grow in intimacy with God. The primary focus in our worship sets is on intimacy with God in our song selection. In our prayer rooms and at conferences, we seek to lead people to have tender encounters with God's heart. We want to write and select songs that the Spirit uses to unlock the deep wells of people's hearts, that they might experience His love.

3.   **Familiar songs:** We encourage worship leaders to select songs that the majority in the room are familiar with so they can engage without having to read the words on the screen for each song. It is helpful not to introduce more than one new song per 2-hour worship set.

4.   **Strong melody line:** We want the people in the room to sing the worship songs. Therefore, we encourage the worship leader to sing a *strong melody line* in the worship songs that they select. This helps people who are not gifted singers to be able to more easily sing the worship song. If the worship leader sings a harmony, rather than the melody line, it is more difficult for the congregation to sing along with them. It is helpful to have at least one singer on melody to help the congregation have confidence to sing along. As a rule, it is also helpful if the worship leader does not ad-lib too much (adding extra notes, words, and embellishments).

5.   **Clear articulation:** Worship leaders should clearly articulate words in the songs.

6.   Leading a known worship song during transition between teams ensures that the singers of the outgoing team keep the song going if there are issues with the sound.

7.   Singers should sing as soon as their mics are on to give others in the room confidence to sing.

B. **Element #2: Spontaneous Singing**

1. The worship team leads the room in singing to God spontaneously both by using the Word and singing in the spirit (1 Cor. 14:15; Eph. 5:19). This part of our model focuses on expressing our affection and adoration to the Lord.

   I will <u>sing with the spirit</u>, and I will also <u>sing with the understanding</u>. (1 Cor. 14:15)

   … speaking to one another in psalms and hymns and spiritual songs, <u>singing and making melody in your heart to the Lord</u>. (Eph. 5:19)

   Let the word of Christ dwell in you … teaching and admonishing one another in psalms and hymns and spiritual songs, <u>singing with grace in your hearts to the Lord</u>. (Col. 3:16)

2. Spontaneous singing indicates the time in intercessory formats for the prayer leader to pray a biblical passage and in the Worship with the Word format for singers to introduce a passage.

3. **Simple chord progressions:** It is important to use *simple* and *basic chord progressions* (not syncopated chord progressions) and to sing in an *easy vocal range* (not high or low notes outside many people's range), so that less-gifted singers in the room can participate.

4. **All singers:** We encourage *all the singers* on the worship team to engage boldly, as this helps others in the room to enter in boldly. The singers should be turned up slightly louder in the room. The blessing of spontaneous singing is in singing the Word and singing in tongues, so we ask the singers not to sing oohs and aahs but to sing the Word or sing in tongues.

5. **Easy melodies:** *Long notes in flowing melodies and harmonies* are preferred to fast or syncopated notes running up and down the scale. Sing in a middle range rather than using mostly high notes or low notes. The worship leader starts with *extended mid-range notes* to give the congregation easy melody lines that help them find melody lines in their own range.

6. **Acoustic guitar:** The acoustic guitar player is encouraged to provide strong rhythmic and melodic support, making it easier for ungifted singers in the room to participate.

7. **Room engagement:** Worship leaders should pay attention to the people in the room to note if they are singing with the worship team. If not, go back to a corporate worship song.

8. **End with a chorus:** The worship leader ends the time of spontaneous singing with a spontaneous chorus ending in a name of God. This is the signal to the prayer leader to pray a biblical passage.

9. We ask that the prayer leader not sing on the microphone during times of spontaneous singing unless they are an approved singer.

10. We ask that the prayer leader not shout over the singers during spontaneous singing.

11. Spontaneous choruses can come out of spontaneous singing.

12. Spontaneous singing can go on for as long or as short as the worship leader feels is appropriate for that moment in the worship cycle.

13. Worship leaders can begin spontaneous singing straight from a worship song or chorus, or they can sing, "Lift your voices to the Lord." Another phrase to use might be, "Sing the love song of your heart to Jesus."

C. *Element #3: Developing a Biblical Passage—Four Parts*

1. **Part 1: Sing or pray through a passage of Scripture**

   a. In the Intercessory Prayer format, the intercessor starts by *reading* a biblical prayer, then prays from that passage for 2–5 minutes.

   b. In the Worship with the Word format, *a singer is to sing through 2–3 verses of a biblical passage* that was selected in the briefing before the worship set began.

   c. We ask the *singers to sing* through the passages instead of the prayer leader speaking out the passages. This gives our singers more opportunity to sing creatively.

2. **Part 2: Isolate a phrase**

   The prayer leader speaks out *one short phrase* from the passage to identify what phrase the singers are to develop with short 3- to 5-second songs.

   a. In the Worship with the Word format, the prayer leader's role is to clearly isolate phrases for the singers, who will flow together in developing their meaning and thus function as a singing seminary. We encourage the prayer leader to limit what they say to a phrase or a short sentence (normally less than 7–8 words). The prayer leader's role is not to teach the passage but to isolate phrases so that *the singers may "teach" or develop the passage together* through short, antiphonal songs.

   b. In Worship with the Word the singers are to participate in developing the passage much more than the prayer leader. The prayer leader should aim to speak at a 1:5 ratio with the singers, (as opposed to a 1:2 ratio in the Intercessory Prayer format).

3. **Part 3: Develop the phrase through antiphonal singing**

   Singers "develop" the phrases by bringing out the meaning of the phrase that is being isolated (or focused on). The singers develop themes from the isolated phrase through antiphonal singing, by taking turns to sing 3- to 5-second songs that expound on the isolated phrase. They do this in three ways:

   a. *Repeat the phrase back:* Sing the *very words* isolated by the prayer leader.

   b. *Paraphrase the phrase:* Sing words that convey a *similar* meaning yet use different words.

   c. *Elaborate on the phrase:* Sing words that *bring out* the meaning of the passage.

4. **Part 4: Sing spontaneous choruses**

   a. The worship leader or chorus leader may sing a spontaneous chorus that is related to the theme of the biblical passage. The chorus leader sings the chorus through twice to establish the melody line, then all the singers are encouraged to sing the chorus in unison boldly to help establish the chorus so that those in the room can quickly join in.

   b. Any singer can offer a chorus by singing the chorus twice. If the chorus is not picked up by the worship leader or chorus leader the singer should not continue to sing it.

    c. All the singers should help carry the melody line in these choruses and, at this time, avoid embellishment or ornamentation or their own songs.

    d. Select easy melodies and sing in a mid-vocal range so that non-musically-gifted people in the congregation can join in quickly. Create choruses that are not too long or complex for those in the room to remember them.

    e. A spontaneous chorus may be sung at any time in the worship cycle—before, during, or after developing a passage. Do not sing the chorus more than 6–7 times. Many might lose interest if the chorus is repeated too much. You may use the same chorus later in the cycle.

    f. The chorus leader ends by singing one of the names of God (e.g., "Oh, God!" or "Father of glory!" etc.) to signal to the rest of the worship team to end the chorus together.

    g. If the prayer leader wants to add 2- to 3-second prayers, we ask that they pray "in the gaps" *between* the choruses instead of shouting over the choruses.

    h. The worship leader or chorus leader may occasionally establish double choruses, in which two different but complementary choruses echo back and forth, answering each other.

D.   ***Element #4: Optional Prayer Activities***

1. **Rapid-fire prayer:** During intercessory prayer, the prayer leader may invite intercessors to come up to pray on the microphone for a specific prayer topic. We call this "rapid-fire prayer," because people pray one after another in quick succession. The theme may cover topics like the government, nations, healing, evangelistic outreaches, university campuses, pro-life themes, etc. We encourage the worship team to keep the music upbeat and energetic.

2. **Small-group prayer:** During Intercessory Prayer formats, the prayer leader may initiate a time to gather in small groups of 4–5 people to pray. The prayer leader should clarify that participation in small-group prayer is optional.

3. **Prayer for the sick:** The prayer leader has the option to make room for a short time of ministry to those who want prayer for physical healing. The prayer leader prays on the microphone for the sick, while those in the room may gather around those who indicate they would like prayer for healing.

4. **Warring in the Spirit:** This may be engaged in at any time in the worship cycle or before, during, or after developing a passage. Singing with an aggressive, militant tone distinguishes it from spontaneous singing, which is a more mellow tone as we express our love and adoration to Jesus. We ask the prayer leaders not to shout over the singers who are warring in the spirit.

V. Developing a Passage—Practical Principles

A. Having a strong beat during antiphonal singing instead of playing quiet background-type music is helpful especially in the Intercessory Prayer format. This helps to sustain team and room participation through 2–3 intercessors.

B. We encourage our teams to continue with the same chord progression from spontaneous singing and gradually change it throughout the antiphonal time and choruses. This will help serve the intercessors and the room by creating a sustained flow from one part of the worship cycle to the next.

C. Selahs can be used to highlight a prophetic moment that is happening musically. The worship leader can sing "selah" to indicate to the prayer leader and singers not to sing or speak until the worship leader indicates the selah is complete (see below for more information).

D. Group singers on the back row (singers 4, 5, and 6) do not antiphonally sing but sing on worship songs and choruses and are encouraged to offer oracles. Having only the front 3 singers (and worship leader) antiphonalizing guards against hesitation that can come from deferring.

E. Sequence of singers: We have a sequence of singers as a way of clearly communicating who should keep singing. The goal of this sequence is to create boldness and confidence in the singers. If two singers start to sing at the same time, one should quickly drop out according to the following order: worship leader, associate worship leader, singer 1, singer 2, singer 3, etc. In other words, if the associate worship leader and singer #3 start to sing at the same time, singer #3 should drop out and defer to the associate worship leader.

1. In the Worship with the Word format, if a singer starts to sing and the prayer leader starts to pray, the prayer leader should defer to the singer.

2. In our Intercessory Prayer format, *the prayer leader has priority over the singers*. In other words, during the antiphonal singing, we ask the singers to pause to allow the prayer leader to participate antiphonally. We do not want the prayer leader to shout over the singers.

3. Sometimes it can be helpful for singers to develop signals to notify the other singers that they have the next short song. Some singers signal one another that they are about to sing by lifting a finger on the hand holding the mic, or they hum a note, or use different signals. If singers keep other singers in their in-ear monitors, they can hear when someone else is about to sing or is slowly humming in preparation to sing.

4. In our Intercessory Prayer format, singer #1 is the first to respond.

5. In Worship with the Word, the singer who has just finished singing through a passage gives the first response after the first isolated phrase.

6. In Worship with the Word, the prayer leader's role is to clearly isolate phrases for the singers, who will flow together in developing their meaning and thus function as a singing seminary. We encourage the prayer leader to limit what they say to a phrase or a short sentence (normally less than 7–8 words). The prayer leader's role is not to teach the passage but to isolate phrases so that *the singers may "teach" or develop the passage* through short, antiphonal songs.

7. In Worship with the Word, the singers are to participate in developing the passage much more than the prayer leader. The prayer leader should aim to speak at a 1:5 ratio with the singers (as opposed to a 1:2 ratio in the Intercessory Prayer format).

VI. Intercessory Prayer Format—Overview

A. In this format, we use biblical prayers or promises—from Jesus, the apostles, or the Old Testament prophets. We intercede for revival for the church across a city or region that the Lord highlights. Or, we focus on specific local, national, or international themes, such as crisis events or political, civil, economic, educational, or family issues, etc.

B. Some prayer meetings have a focus that is set by the GPR leadership team, however, intercessors may pray for any subject or theme even in prayer meetings that have a focus.

C. **_Worship Cycle 1:_** About 45 minutes

    1. _Corporate worship_—about 20 minutes

    2. _Spontaneous singing_—about 2–3 minutes

    3. _Intercession_—three intercessors (their prayer may be developed with antiphonal singing)

    4. _Optional prayers_—rapid fire, small group, for the sick, warring in the spirit

D. **_Worship Cycles 2, 3, 4:_** About 20–30 minutes each

    1. _Corporate worship_—about 5 minutes

    2. _Spontaneous singing_—about 2–3 minutes

    3. _Intercession_—three intercessors (their prayer may be developed with antiphonal singing)

    4. _Optional_—rapid-fire prayer, small-group prayer, warring in the spirit

E. Worship leader responsibilities: The worship leader takes the lead on song selection, determining the number of worship songs in each cycle, the length of singing spontaneously, when prophetic oracles and musical selahs are released, and more.

F. The prayer leader typically prays first in the first cycle. After that, the prayer leader simply nods at the next intercessor sitting in the chairs waiting to pray on the mic to indicate that is time for them to go to the mic. As a rule, three intercessors will pray in each cycle. The prayer leader does not need to confer with the worship leader, but simply allows for three intercessors plus the option of one of the following—rapid-fire prayer, small-group prayer, prayer for the sick, or warring in the spirit.

VII. Worship With the Word Format—Overview

A. The purpose of the Worship with the Word format is to provide our singers an opportunity to grow in the Word and thus to function as a singing seminary by singing a psalm or another portion of Scripture. This format provides a context for worship teams to be creative and to grow in prophetic singing while providing an anointed atmosphere in the prayer room for others to prayerfully read the Word.

B. *Worship Cycle 1:* About 30–40 minutes

   1. *Corporate worship*—about 15–20 minutes

   2. *Spontaneous singing*—about 2–3 minutes

   3. *Developing a biblical passage* (through antiphonal singing)—about 10–20 minutes

C. *Worship Cycles 2, 3, 4:* About 20–30 minutes each

   1. *Corporate worship*—about 5 minutes

   2. *Spontaneous singing*—about 2–3 minutes

   3. *Developing a biblical passage* (through antiphonal singing)—about 10–20 minutes

VIII. Example of Developing a Passage—Intercessory Prayer Format

A. *Part 1: Pray through a Biblical Passage*

   1. The intercessor starts by reading the biblical passage and then prays for 2–5 minutes. Intercessors are to pray biblical prayers (see "Praying Biblical Prayers" below).

   2. Example of praying Ephesians 3:16–18

   [16] That He would grant you … to be strengthened with might through His Spirit in the inner man, [17] that Christ may dwell in your hearts through faith; that you, being rooted and grounded in love, [18] may be able to comprehend with all the saints what is the width and length and depth and height … (Eph. 3:16–18)

B. *Part 2: Isolate a Phrase*

1. After the intercessor has finished praying for 2–5 minutes, he or she may isolate a phrase from the passage. They may say, *"in the name of Jesus,"* before the phrase they are isolating to make it clear to the singers which phrase to develop with 3- to 5-second antiphonal songs.

2. Two examples of isolating phrases from Ephesians 3:16–18:

3. Example A: *"Strengthen them with might through Your Spirit in the inner man."*

4. Example B: *". . . that they may be rooted and grounded in love."*

C. *Part 3: Develop a Phrase through Antiphonal Singing*

1. For example: *"Strengthen them with might through Your Spirit in the inner man."*

2. Repeat the phrase back: *"Strengthen them with might through Your Spirit."*

3. Paraphrase the phrase: *"Release Your power to their inner man."*

4. Elaborate on the phrase: *"Impart grace to cause their hearts to flow in love."*

D. *Part 4: Spontaneous Choruses*

1. For example: *"Release a greater measure of Your strength in them by Your Spirit."*

IX. Example of Developing a Passage—Worship with the Word Format

A. *Part 1: Sing through a Biblical Passage*

For example, one may sing Psalm 45:1–4, omitting some phrases. The singer is free to "edit" the passage by skipping or adding a few words to make the passage easier to sing and to help the people in the room understand the passage.

[1] My heart is overflowing with a good theme ... concerning the King ... [2] You are fairer [more beautiful] *than the sons of men; grace is poured upon Your lips ... [3] Gird Your sword upon Your thigh, O Mighty One ... [4] In Your majesty ride prosperously* [victoriously] *because of truth, humility, and righteousness. (Ps. 45:1–4)*

B. **Part 2: Isolate a Phrase**

The prayer leader speaks out one phrase from Psalm 45:1–4 to indicate for the singers what phrase is to be developed with short three- to five-second songs.

Examples of isolating phrases from Psalm 45:1–4:

1. Example A: *"Jesus, You are more beautiful than the sons of men."*

2. Example B: *"In Your majesty go forth victoriously for the cause of humility."*

C. **Part 3: Develop a Phrase through Antiphonal Singing**

Examples of developing the phrase, *"Jesus, You are more beautiful than the sons of men"*:

1. Repeat the phrase back: *"Jesus, You are more beautiful than the sons of men."*

2. Paraphrase the phrase: *"Jesus, Your splendor and majesty move my heart."*

3. Elaborate on the phrase: *"Holy Spirit, show us how beautiful His love is."*

D. **Part 4: Spontaneous Choruses**

1. Example of a chorus: *"Holy Spirit, fascinate the Church with Jesus' beauty."*

X. Leadership Responsibilities—Intercessory Prayer Format

A. **Worship Leader Responsibilities**

The worship leader selects songs and determines the length of spontaneous singing and choruses and when oracles and musical selahs are released, etc.

B. **Prayer Leader Responsibilities**

The prayer leader has three people intercede on the mic per cycle and exercises the options of having rapid-fire prayer, small-group prayer, or prayer for the sick.

1. The prayer leader does not need to communicate with the worship leader to have three intercessors pray in a row nor to get permission to end a cycle with rapid-fire prayer, small-group prayer, or prayer for the sick. These are standard parts of the structure that the worship leader expects to happen.

2. The prayer leader should not arrange the intercessors in a specific order but allow the intercessors to simply pray in the order in which they sit in the chairs. It is okay if an intercessor prays on a different theme than the intercessor before them.

XI. Leadership Responsibilities—Worship with the Word Format

A. *Worship Leader Responsibilities*

The worship leader selects songs and determines the passage to sing through, the length of spontaneous singing, and when oracles and musical selahs are released, etc.

1. Worship leaders make a scripture passage outline, indicating the verses that they have selected for each worship cycle. They select biblical passages with phrases from which it is easy to express heart responses to God. Some phrases or verses that are hard to sing may be omitted. A copy of the scripture passage outline should be given to each singer.

2. The worship leader may choose to use the same passage and worship outline for 4–6 weeks, so that the team will have an opportunity to study the passage in more depth.

3. The singers should sing through the passage to introduce it instead of the prayer leader reading the passage on the mic.

4. At the end of a cycle, if the antiphonal singing is flowing along a strong theme and the worship leader thinks they will lose momentum by changing the music (i.e. by singing a new worship song), he or she has the option to start the new worship cycle with a spontaneous chorus or double chorus instead of a corporate worship song.

B. *Prayer Leader Responsibilities* (includes isolating a phrase)

1. The prayer leader has a support role in this format. Their main function is to keep *the isolated phrase obvious* to the singers—to give the singers a clear target at which to aim as they develop the passage.

2. The prayer leader should not read the passage on the mic to introduce it but rather have the singers sing through the passage.

3. The prayer leader's role is *not* to teach the passage, but to isolate phrases so that the singers may "teach" or develop the passage together through short antiphonal songs. We encourage prayer leaders to only say short phrases (7–8 words or less).

4. The prayer leader should aim to isolate 3–4 different phrases from a biblical passage in each worship cycle.

XII. Using Biblical Prayers

A. We ask all prayer leaders to use the prayers of the Bible when praying on the microphone. Biblical prayers are not the same as praying Bible "exhortations." Some who pray Bible exhortations instead of Bible prayers are tempted to exhort and preach the Bible exhortation—with their eyes closed as if praying—on the microphone.

B. The prayers of the Bible include the following characteristics:

1. **Praying for the release of the Spirit's activity:** Pray for the release of the activity of the Spirit (e.g., increase of love, holiness, power, wisdom, understanding, perseverance, unity, etc.). Seek to avoid "preaching prayers" that exhort the people in the prayer room to obey and repent. In other words, focus on talking to God instead of exhorting people in the room.

2. **Praying positive prayers:** The New Testament prayers focus on the impartation of positive virtues like love, holiness, unity, and faith instead of focusing on the removal of negative things like sin, division, lust, or demons. Praying for the impartation of positive virtues helps the believers in the prayer room to be unity with one another, whereas negative prayers often have an opposite effect.

3. **Praying God-centered prayers:** All NT prayers are directed to and focused on God instead of on speaking to the devil or addressing or describing various sins.

4. **Praying for the whole church in the city:** The prayers of the NT are mostly focused on the release of the Spirit's activity on the whole church in a specific city.

C. We ask the intercessors to limit their prayer on the microphone to five to seven minutes total in order to give others the opportunity to pray.

D. If the intercessor wants to involve the singers, then he or she *simply pauses* to make room for the singers by saying "in the name of Jesus" before a phrase that they isolate. The intercessor then continues to offer five- to ten-second prayers that flow in an antiphonal way with the singers, aiming for a 1:2 ratio of intercessor interjections to antiphonal songs. However, the intercessor does not have to involve the singers.

E. We ask the singers to make room for the intercessor to offer short phrases, so that the intercessor can pray in the gaps instead of shouting over the singers.

XIII. Briefings and Transitions

A. *Briefing*

The purpose of the briefing is to prepare for the set. We ask that all members of the worship team arrive thirty minutes before their worship set begins to maximize the time available. The briefing should end ten minutes before the hour in order for transition to begin on time.

B. *Transition*

The section leaders are to pay attention to each transition and speak into it to ensure that the transition happens smoothly according to how the GPR leadership team has determined.

1. The team admin for the outgoing team should check with the incoming team during their briefing to determine and communicate what instrument the incoming worship leader is using.

2. The new worship leader should *go on the stage ten minutes before the hour.* At this time all the singers and musicians on the incoming team should also go out to stand in the backstage area *as soon as* the worship leader leaves the briefing room to go on stage.

3. When the new worship leader comes on stage, the group singers (4, 5, and 6) for the outgoing team should exit, and the group singers for the incoming team should come on.

4. If the outgoing worship leader is on the same instrument as the incoming worship leader, by default the *chorus leader* of the outgoing team is responsible to lead the worship song. The chorus leader should sing a worship song (teams should have a list of predetermined transition songs)—sometimes they will not start this new worship song after a lively chorus ends.

5. The incoming worship leader will give the exiting worship leader (or the chorus leader leading a worship song) a nod when they are ready to go.

6. The incoming worship leader should not nod until their RSS is adjusted properly, their instrument is tuned and ready, and they are ready to immediately sing their transition song.

7. The exiting singers should stay until they are sure the new worship leader's mic and instrument are working. If the oncoming worship leader has any trouble with their instrument or sound, the chorus leader of the outgoing team is responsible for singing a worship song until the worship leader and sound tech have resolved the issue.

8. Once the incoming worship leader is singing, then the exiting singers can leave. At that time the incoming primary singers (1, 2, and 3) come on stage, and the musicians should begin to transition (outgoing musicians tear down, incoming musicians set up).

9. The incoming worship leader should begin singing a known worship song instead of only playing their instrument for an extended period of time.

XIV. Why We Pray in a Moderate Volume on the Microphone

A. We ask those praying on the microphone to pray in a moderate volume as a general rule. We are not asking to do away with high volume altogether, but, as a rule, we ask that people pray at a moderate volume instead of shouting their prayer. We request this for a few reasons.

1. **First**, most people are not able to shout on a microphone—they have neither the personality nor the voice for it. Therefore, *they do not feel welcome* to pray on the microphone if the unspoken standard of "anointed prayer" is shouting. They draw back, feeling like they are being judged as unanointed and lacking passion in prayer.

   a. We want all to have confidence to pray on the microphone in our prayer room, even those with a quieter personality.

   b. We encourage our intercessors to model praying in a moderate volume for the sake of many (in the room and who watch our web steam) who want to pray on the mic, but do not have confidence to do so if they feel that they have to shout.

2. **Second**, some erroneously believe that shouting their prayers means that they are more passionate and anointed and are therefore making a greater impact in the Spirit. However, spiritual authority is not determined by the volume or speed of our prayers, but it is based on the authority of Jesus and His finished work on the cross.

3. **Third**, God is our Father and He has tender love for us. Therefore, we can approach Him with confidence that He hears us because He delights in us and in our prayers that agree with His heart and Word. We do not need to beg Him in a whiney tone, nor shout at Him in a preaching tone, hoping to convince Him to hear us. Because He loves we can approach Him in tender love with confidence that He has already opened His heart to us.

4. **Fourth**, many have asked us to encourage people not to shout on the microphone because it hurts their ears. Some have to leave the prayer room if the volume is too loud. It makes the prayer room uncomfortable, instead of engaging and enjoyable.

B. We must remember that we are addressing our Father who loves and enjoys us as His children. So, *we would not normally shout at our Father in a preaching tone but speak to Him with confidence in a tone of faith and affection, since He delights in our prayers.* We come boldly yet with tender love to agree with His heart rather than to try to convince Him to do what He is reluctant to do.

XV. Stage and Sound Booth Etiquette

A. Both stage and sound booth etiquette include having only water present.

B. All beverages in the sound booth must be in a closed container. We ask the sound techs not to bring food to the sound booth.

C. Talkback mic—the talkback is used to help team communication during the set and is to be used minimally (only when absolutely necessary). Values behind limiting use of the talkback mic are as follows:

1. Giving the musicians the ability to grow in improvisational skills and development through listening rather than constant instruction

2. Worship leaders growing in their ability to lead through vocal cues and hand signals

3. Not wanting to distract from the worship set by overuse of talkback mic, thus creating a context for overfamiliarity and joking

XVI. When the Sound System Stops Working

A. We ask all the singers and musicians to be alert in the rare occasions when the sound system does not work for a few minutes. The sound techs and the section leader will work to fix it. *We ask the entire worship team to continue going strong, even without electricity.* The "fire on the altar" must not ever go out on your watch.

B. By the grace of God, we have never stopped the music since September 19, 1999, so we entrust each worship team to be very serious to keep the fire going on their watch. For this, the IHOPKC leadership team is immensely grateful.

4

Enjoyable Prayer—Sixteen Values of the Harp and Bowl Model

The Lord desires that His people experience joy in prayer, that is, *enjoyable prayer* (Isa. 56:7). The only type of prayer that will be sustained night and day is *enjoyable prayer*. Prayer is more enjoyable when we encounter the love and beauty of God that tenderizes and fascinates our heart and when it is combined with anointed music and prophetic singers.

> *⁷ Even them I will bring to My holy mountain, and make them joyful in My house of prayer. (Isa. 56:7)*

Value #1. Growing in Intimacy with Our Beautiful God

1. King David gave insight into how to experience enjoyable prayer (Ps. 27:4; 37:4; 149:4). His lifelong preoccupation was to behold the beauty of God, especially His beauty that is manifest in His affections toward His people. David wrote of God's pleasure in His people.

    > *⁴ One thing I have desired of the Lord … to behold the beauty of the Lord. (Ps. 27:4)*
    > *⁴ For the Lord takes pleasure in His people. (Ps. 149:4)*

2. Our primary focus in worship is on interacting tenderly with God as our Father and Jesus as our Bridegroom King, rather than on our failure and sin, or resisting the work of the devil. Yes, we repent of our sin and resist the enemy, but these are not the focus of enjoyable prayer.

Value #2. Combining Worship and Intercession

1. Worship and intercession flow together at God's throne (Rev. 4–5). The twenty-four elders each have a harp and bowl—the *harp* speaks of music and songs, and the *bowls* represent prayers to God.

    > *⁸ The twenty-four elders … each having a harp, and golden bowls full of incense, which are the prayers of the saints. (Rev. 5:8)*

2. There is increased enjoyment in prayer when it is offered to God in a context where there is anointed worship and prophetic singing.

Value #3. Praying in the Spirit and Spontaneous Singing

1. Prayer is more enjoyable when we cultivate a flowing heart—this is enhanced by singing spontaneously. This commonly occurs by singing with our spirit and with our understanding.

    ¹⁵ I will sing with the spirit, and I will also sing with the understanding. (1 Cor. 14:15)

2. Singing with our spirit means singing in tongues (1 Cor. 14:2–4), and singing with our understanding includes spontaneously singing the Word from our heart (Eph. 5:19; Col. 3:16).

    ¹⁹ ... speaking to one another in psalms and hymns and spiritual songs, <u>singing and making melody in your heart to the Lord.</u> (Eph. 5:19)

    ¹⁶ Let the <u>word of Christ</u> dwell in you richly ... teaching and admonishing one another in psalms and hymns and spiritual songs, <u>singing with grace</u> in your hearts to the Lord. (Col. 3:16)

Value #4. Cultivating a Prophetic Spirit on Singers and Musicians

1. Enjoyable prayer includes prayer led by the Holy Spirit prophetically inspiriting the singers and musicians. The Lord created us with a longing for music. Anointed music and singing touch the deepest places in our heart and help to unify God's people. For example, in a stadium of 100,000 people, a preacher could *say*, "God loves you," and some would feel the power of that truth. But a worship team could *sing* of God's love, and thousands could feel the power of that truth in a deeper way. Through anointed worship songs, thousands can be unified as *they feel the same thing* by singing the same thing to the *same Man.*

2. King David was intentional about investing time and money into training musicians and singers to flow in the prophetic spirit while ministering in the tabernacle (1 Chr. 25:1–3).

    ¹David ... separated for the service some of the sons of Asaph, of Heman, and of Jeduthun, who should <u>prophesy with harps</u>, stringed instruments, and cymbals ... ² The sons of Asaph ... <u>prophesied with a harp</u> to give thanks and to praise the Lord. (1 Chr. 25:1–3)

3. Harps, string instruments, trumpets, and other instruments (1 Chr. 16:42), were important in David's ministry (2 Sam. 6:15; 1 Chr. 13:8; 15:24, 28; 16:6, 42; cf. 2 Chr. 5:12–13; 7:6; 13:12, 14; 15:14; 20:28; 23:13; 29:26–28; Ezra 3:10; Neh. 4:20; 12:35, 41; Ps. 98:5-6; 150:3).

4. When King Jehoshaphat asked the prophet Elisha for the word of the Lord, Elisha asked for a musician to play so that the hand of the Lord would come upon him to prophesy to the king.

> *15 "But now bring me a <u>musician</u>." Then it happened, <u>when the musician played</u>, that the hand of the LORD came upon him. (2 Kgs. 3:15)*

Value #5. Antiphonal Singing and Team Ministry in Prayer with Worship

1. Enjoyable prayer includes experiencing the joy of creativity in the context of team ministry. This can be enhanced by singers flowing together in antiphonal singing with a prayer leader. In other words, antiphonal singing or responsive singing can be a dynamic expression of team ministry, and it often results in a greater flow of the Spirit in the worship team.

2. David established responsive or antiphonal singing between individual singers and between choirs (Ezra 3:10-11; Neh. 12:24).

> *11 And they <u>sang responsively</u>, praising and giving thanks to the LORD. (Ezra 3:11)*
>
> *24 The heads of the Levites were ... with their brothers <u>across from them</u>, to praise and give thanks, <u>group alternating with group</u>, according to the command of David ... 31 I ... appointed two <u>large thanksgiving</u> choirs. (Neh. 12:24, 31)*

3. Thanksgiving psalms were possibly sung responsively to one another.

> *8 Jeshua, Binnui, Kadmiel, Sherebiah, Judah ... <u>led the thanksgiving psalms</u> ... 9 Also Bakbukiah and Unni, their brethren, <u>stood across from them in their duties</u>. (Neh. 12:8–9)*

4. Worship around God's throne is antiphonal—note the five responses of various groups as they minister to God as one team in Revelation 5. First the living creatures and elders sing (5:8–10); then myriads of angels join them (5:11–12); then all creation joins in (5:13); the living creatures cry out in a chorus of "Amen!" (5:14); and the elders break out into worship (5:14).

> *8 ... the <u>four living creatures</u> and the <u>twenty-four elders</u> ... 9 they sang a new song, saying: "You are worthy to take the scroll ... for You were slain, and have redeemed us to God ..." 11 Then I looked, and I heard the voice of many angels around the throne ... 12 saying with a loud voice: "Worthy is the Lamb who was slain to receive power and riches and wisdom, and strength and honor and glory and blessing!" 13 And <u>every creature</u> which is in heaven and on the earth ... I heard saying: "Blessing and honor and glory and power be to Him who sits on the throne, and to the Lamb ..." 14 Then the <u>four living creatures</u> said, "Amen!" And the twenty-four elders fell down and worshiped Him who lives forever and ever. (Rev. 5:8–14)*

Value #6. Structure in Prayer Meetings

1. We designed the structure in our prayer model to facilitate participating with the spontaneous flow of the Spirit in our songs and music, resulting in greater creativity and making prayer enjoyable. We can experience a more spontaneous flow of the Spirit within the boundaries of a clearly established structure, if the structure is designed properly.

2. Our model is primarily a *communication tool* that enables our singers, musicians, worship leader, and prayer leader to flow together boldly without timidity or hesitation. The structure identifies the times and ways when various members of the team have liberty to be more creative with their instrument or voice.

3. The structure in our prayer model is a *permission-giving mechanism* that leads to spontaneity by dismantling fear in the singers and musicians. The structure empowers them with confidence to step out in new and creative ways that are affirmed in the model. Clearly defined roles, options, and expectations lead to greater boldness, confidence, and unity for the members of a worship team to express themselves in ways that are agreed upon by all.

4. Our structure identifies the places where our singers and musicians have options to be creative—they include instrumental and vocal improvisation, antiphonal singing, prophetic oracles, the length of a worship cycle, the choice of the passage to develop, the selection of worship songs, modes of prayer (devotionals, intercession, ministry time), prophetic themes, spontaneous singing, singing solos, and length and style of prophetic musical selahs.

5. Fear paralyzes the flow of the prophetic spirit in a worship team. The fear of being judged by others for expressing ourselves in a wrong way hinders the confidence to flow together in the Spirit. This model minimizes the fear of being too domineering or too timid. Fear, timidity, or lack of confidence hinder singers and musicians from flowing in the Spirit. Being preoccupied with the fear of "missing God" or of doing something that their worship team will not appreciate hinders singers and musicians. These are minimized via the model.

6. Compare the structure in our model to the relationship between ski jumper and the ski ramp. The skier goes down the long ski ramp, preparing to jump and soaring high into the air. When they are finished making the jump, they get back on the ski ramp and prepare to jump again.

a. This is similar to when a worship team is inspired by the Spirit and "soars high" with spontaneous music. When the spontaneous prophetic flow ends, then we "land" within the structure (by going back to singing a few familiar worship songs) as we anticipate taking another "jump" from the ramp into more spontaneous flow of the Spirit.

b. When a worship team is engaged with the Spirit and soaring high, we do not want them to quench the flow to return to the structure (ski ramp). However, when the spontaneous prophetic flow ends, then we "land on" the structure, ready to launch out again.

7. The Lord has combined structure with spontaneity in many places in creation. For example, precise, predictable order exists in our solar system alongside spontaneous, unpredictable air currents. The human skeletal structure supports a spontaneous flow of air, fluids, and blood.

Value #7. Platform Ministry Style—Humility and Exalting Jesus

1. We value a platform ministry style in which people express themselves in a spirit of humility and genuineness that exalts Jesus. Thus, a platform ministry style that draws attention to Jesus and not to the people ministering on the platform. The Spirit is zealous to exalt Jesus.

   14 "He will glorify Me, for He [Spirit] will take of what is Mine and declare it ..." (Jn. 16:14)

2. Paul was zealous to preach Jesus and not draw attention to himself.

   5 For we do not preach ourselves, but Christ Jesus ... (2 Cor. 4:5)

3. In the secular entertainment industry, some develop their personal "signature platform moves" to draw more attention to themselves and to distinguish themselves from other performers. We ask our teachers, singers, and musicians to avoid being *overly* expressive by waving hands and arms and more, or by *imitating* what appears to be manifestations of the Spirit, or by other *heightened* vocal or physical expressions that draw attention to them. In conferences, when there are crowds, *we lead on the stage in the same way that we lead on it in our prayer room.*

4. It is common today to see preachers and worship leaders engage in various platform theatrics, exhibitionism, and showmanship that draw undue attention to themselves. We encourage all who minister on our platform in teaching or singing to refrain from hype in what they say and from expressing themselves in overly animated ways that draw attention to themselves.

5.   We ask our teams to be genuine in how they express themselves by *not doing publicly* what they do not *regularly do in their private devotion to Jesus*. Some express themselves spiritually on stage (when the lights are bright and crowds are big) differently than they do when the room is nearly empty or when they are alone with Jesus—this type of showmanship is common today.

6.   We do not do worship sets to entertain people, but to invoke a spirit of adoration of the King as we worship and contend in prayer for the breakthrough of revival. Whether in the GPR or hosting a conference, we want to be in line with our divine assignment as a ministry—to carry ourselves with a spirit of humility as we seek to exalt Jesus and draw others to do so.

7.   The IHOPKC leadership rejoices to see how our worship teams have excelled in this for years. Visiting leaders often comment on the humility in the platform ministry style in the GPR and at our conferences and on the absence of hype and a spirit of performance in our worship teams.

8.   We are making a prophetic statement when ***we do not change what we do*** when on a stage with a big crowd—we do the same things when there is a big crowd as we do when there are only a few in the prayer room. We do not change, because we focus on ministering to Jesus.

9.   Some worship movements seem to take their cues from the secular music industry. It is best to take our cue from the worship around the throne (Rev. 4) where none seek to draw attention to themselves. Many houses of prayer take their cues from us. Thus, we want to serve as an encouragement to those groups to maintain a spirit of humility and excellence in this area.

10.   We value a platform ministry style that refuses to exaggerate the Spirit's activity and refuses to manipulate a response in others that is not genuine. For some, this may involve being more restrained than what they were accustomed to in their previous ministry involvement.

11.   John the Baptist described himself as a "friend of the bridegroom". A friend of the Bridegroom parallels the best man in a wedding who wants the bride to focus on her bridegroom instead of seeking to win the affections of the bride himself.

> [29] **"The friend of the bridegroom** ... *rejoices greatly because of the bridegroom's voice. Therefore this joy of mine is fulfilled.* [30] *He must increase, but I must decrease."* (Jn. 3:29–30)

12. When we minister in the spirit of a friend of the Bridegroom we are at peace when others less dedicated and gifted than us receive the recognition and opportunities that we may deserve.

Value #8. God-Centered Spiritual Warfare

1. The New Testament presents engaging in spiritual warfare with a God-centered focus. The New Testament distinguishes between two categories of demonic spirits—spirits who dwell *in people* and demonic spirits that dwell *in heavenly places*, or demonic principalities (Eph. 6:12). As a rule, we *directly rebuke spirits* that dwell in people, but *resist* principalities in the heavens by *directly addressing God*. There are exceptions to this general rule.

2. We engage in spiritual warfare by agreeing with God and disagreeing with the enemy. When agreeing with who He is and what He promises to do preoccupies us, our faith is stirred and much prayer is sustainable and enjoyable.

   a. *Worship is agreement with **who God is***. In worship, we declare truths about God. For example, we may say or sing to God, "You are worthy! You are holy! You are good!"

   b. *Intercession is agreement with **what God promises to do***. For example, we may pray, "Lord, release Your Spirit in a greater measure and send revival," and so on.

   c. *Repentance is coming into agreement **with God's character***. In repentance, we express sorrow for our sins and affirm our desire to walk in holiness, love, and humility—we break agreement with darkness and come into agreement with God's character.

   d. *Prayer for the sick is coming into agreement **with God's compassion***. We break any of our agreement with sickness and ask for the release of God's compassion through healing.

3. The intercessory prayers in the New Testament are God-centered. All of the approximately twenty-five prayers of the apostles are directed to God. None are directed at the devil or sin. Our *primary* focus is to offer God-centered prayers rather than demon- or sin-focused prayers, though on specific occasions the Spirit may lead us to stand against a principality in a direct way.

Value #9. Praying Biblical Prayers

1. Biblical prayers are the prayers that are recorded in the Scripture. They are the language of God's heart. We encourage people to focus on *praying to God* and to avoid "preaching prayers" that *exhort people* in the prayer room by explaining their need to repent.

2. The prayers in the New Testament are *positive prayers*. They focus on asking God to release good qualities rather than asking Him to remove negative activities. Paul prayed that the Lord would release love, faith, unity, peace, righteousness, and power rather than asking the Lord to remove hate, division, fear, sin, etc. We believe that the positive focus of NT prayers was designed by God to make it easier for His people to be united in prayer meetings instead of being judgmental of those who pray negative prayers that seem to criticize the body of Christ.

3. Identificational repentance, as done by Ezra (Ezra 9:6–15) and Nehemiah (Neh. 1:6–9), is effective when the Spirit orchestrates it at key moments in history and when it is led by those in positions of authority with responsibility over the people that they are confessing the sin of—Ezra and Nehemiah were in the primary leadership of the Jews in the land of Israel.

Value #10. The Joy of Answered Prayer

1. Enjoyable prayer includes experiencing the joy of seeing our specific prayers answered by God. It moves us deeply when the God of heaven specifically answers our specific prayer requests. It confirms to us that He hears us and that our prayers and words move His heart.

   ²⁴ "Ask, and you will receive, <u>that your joy may be full.</u>" (Jn. 16:24)

2. We experience joy by seeing answers to our specific prayers for the sick, or for specific miracles, or breakthroughs in specific ways for our friends and family or our city, etc.

Value #11. The Joy of Evangelism

1. Enjoyable prayer includes the joy of seeing unbelievers come to the Lord. It brings great joy to us when we connect the salvation of souls with our prayers for the harvest.

    3 ... describing the conversion of the Gentiles; and they <u>caused great joy</u> to all the brethren. (Acts 15:3)

    10 " ... <u>there is joy</u> in the presence of the angels of God <u>over one sinner who repents</u>." (Lk. 15:10)

2. One of the great joys to be experienced in the end-time prayer movement is found in engaging in prayer that allows the intercessors to see and participate in end-time harvesttime.

Value #12. Joy in Loving the Whole Church

1. Enjoyable prayer includes experiencing the joy of loving the whole Church and laboring together in unity across various denominations and cultures. Paul experienced joy in seeing unity among the believers across a city and throughout the nations.

    2 Fulfill my joy by being like-minded, having the same love, being of one accord. (Phil. 2:2)

2. The Lord only releases the fullness of His purpose in the context of "all the saints":

    18 ... may be able to comprehend <u>with all the saints</u> what is the width and length and depth and height— 19 to know the love of Christ which passes knowledge; that you may be <u>filled with all the fullness of God</u>. (Eph. 3:18–19)

3. We find joy in prayer as we pray for the whole Church to be unified and blessed.

    1 Behold, how good and how pleasant it is for brethren to dwell together in unity! ... 3 for there the Lord commanded the blessing. (Ps. 133:1–3)

Value #13. Perseverance—Staying Engaged in Prayer

1. We value perseverance in prayer. This has two different expressions. First, by the grace of God we continue to contend for God's promises even when the fullness of a promise is delayed (Lk. 11:5–10). He withholds a measure of blessing until His people persevere in prayer.

   5 He said to them, "Which of you shall have a friend, and go to him at midnight and say to him, 'Friend, lend me three loaves; 6 for a friend of mine has come to me on his journey ...' 7 and he will answer from within and say, 'Do not trouble me; the door is now shut, and my children are with me in bed ...'? 8 I say to you ... because of his <u>persistence</u> he will rise and give him as many as he needs. 9 So I say to you, ask, and <u>it will be given to you</u>; seek, and you will find; knock, and <u>it will be opened to you</u>." (Lk. 11:5–9)

2. Second, during prayer meetings, we seek to persevere in engaging with God as others pray, and we resist our tendency to be distracted by a wandering mind. Perseverance in prayer for breakthrough is an expression of love.

   18 ... praying always with all prayer and supplication in the Spirit, being watchful to this end <u>with all perseverance</u> and supplication for all the saints. (Eph. 6:18)

3. It is easy to be disengaged in a prayer meeting. Blessing is related to "stirring ourselves up" to overcome being tired and distracted and to not giving up until God's promises are released.

   7 And there is no one who calls on Your name, <u>who stirs himself up to take hold of You</u> ... (Isa. 64:7)

Value #14. Militant Boldness against the Works of Darkness

1. Jesus came to earth to destroy the works of the devil (1 Jn. 3:8).

   8 For this purpose ... [Jesus] was manifested, that <u>He might destroy the works of the devil</u>. (1 Jn. 3:8)

2. Satan is our enemy who seeks to destroy us. We must not be passive about resisting him.

   8 Your <u>adversary the devil</u> walks about like a roaring lion, <u>seeking whom he may devour</u>. (1 Pet. 5:8)

   7 Therefore submit to God. <u>Resist the devil</u> and he will flee from you. (Jas. 4:7)

3.   We are called to boldly stand in faith and wrestle against demonic activity (Eph. 6:10–13).

> *¹¹ Put on the whole armor of God, that you may be able to <u>stand against</u> the … devil. ¹² For we do not <u>wrestle against</u> flesh and blood, but against principalities … (Eph. 6:11–12)*

4.   We can have both a militant spirit with a bold stand and a tender spirit of devotion to Jesus. The main issue in having a militant boldness in our faith is in knowing that Jesus has already won the victory. Our confidence in prayer is based on the authority that we all have freely received in Christ, the power of God's Word, and His tender love for us. Some confuse boldness to stand against the enemy with shouting at the devil with emotional fervor.

Value #15. Faith for a Revival and a Victorious Church

1.   When faith for revival runs high, then zeal for persevering prayer also runs high. Believing God for an historic breakthrough of revival according to His promise is essential fuel to persevering prayer. By understanding the promises in God's Word for a great end-time revival (along with the testimony of various revivals in history) we are empowered to not draw back in the passivity of being content with the low measure of God's manifest power seen in the Church.

2.   In the Scripture, the Lord promised a great revival for the end-time church. The end-time revival will surpass all other revivals in history (Eph. 5:27; Acts 2:17–21), resulting in a purified church and a great harvest of souls from all nations (Rev. 7:9, 14; 19:7).

> *⁷ ". . . for the marriage of the Lamb has come, and <u>His wife has made herself ready</u>." (Rev. 19:7)*

> *¹⁷ "'And it shall come to pass in the last days, says God, that <u>I will pour out of My Spirit on all flesh</u>; your sons and your daughters shall prophesy … ¹⁸ And on My menservants and on My maidservants I will pour out My Spirit … ¹⁹ I will show <u>wonders in heaven</u> above and <u>signs in the earth</u> beneath: blood and fire and vapor of smoke.'" (Acts 2:17–19)*

> *⁹ I looked, and behold, a <u>great multitude</u> which no one could number, of all nations, tribes, peoples, and tongues, standing before the throne and before the Lamb … (Rev. 7:9)*

3.   Many examples throughout church history can stir our faith as we see that the Lord released an unusual measure of the Holy Spirit's activity in response to persevering prayer. For example, the First and Second Great Awakenings in America were

preceded by much prayer. By reading the testimony of what the Spirit did in those two seasons of great revival, our faith is stirred to contend for a third Great Awakening in our nation.

a. The First Great Awakening (around 1730–1755) is associated with the preaching of George Whitefield, Jonathan Edwards, John Wesley, and others.

b. The Second Great Awakening (around 1790–1840) is associated with the preaching of Charles Finney, Peter Cartwright, Francis Asbury, and others.

Value #16. Prayer That Both Stops God's Judgments and Releases Them on the Antichrist's Empire

1. The Lord will use the prayers of the saints in two very different ways—to stop God's judgments on the nations and to release God's judgments on the Antichrist's empire.

2. The saints are exhorted to pray for great mercy, that the Lord would withhold His judgments on cities and nations and heal the land (2 Chr. 7:14; Jer. 18:7–8; Joel 2:12–17; Zeph. 2:1–3).

14 "If __My people__ ... will humble themselves, and __pray and seek My face__, and turn from their wicked ways, then I will hear ... and will forgive their sin and __heal their land__." (2 Chr. 7:14)

12 "__Turn to Me with all your heart__, with fasting, with weeping ..." 13 Return to the Lord ... for He is gracious and merciful ... and of great kindness; and __He relents from doing harm__. (Joel 2:12–13)

3. The Lord searches for intercessors who pray for His judgments to be withheld (Ezek. 22:30).

30 "So __I sought for a man__ among them who would make a wall, and __stand in the gap__ before Me on behalf of the land, that __I should not destroy it__; but I found no one." (Ezek. 22:30)

4. During the Great Tribulation, the Body of Christ will partner with Jesus in prayer as He releases His judgments to stop the Antichrist's oppression and wickedness (Rev. 8:3–5). The saints are *only* to pray for these judgments after the Great Tribulation begins, and *only* on the Antichrist's empire. The prayers of "all" the saints are both those that are accumulated from history as well as those offered in the generation in which the Lord returns.

3 Then another angel ... was given much incense, that he should offer it with the __prayers of all the saints__ ... 4 The smoke of the incense, with the __prayers of the saints__, ascended before God. (Rev. 8:3–4)

5

WHAT WE DO IN OUR PRAYER ROOM

I. Why We Keep a 24/7 Sanctuary of Prayer with Worship

A. We keep a 24/7 sanctuary to minister to God, release His power through prayer and worship, and encounter His heart. In prayer, we contend for a breakthrough of power in our own hearts, in ministry, and in revelation.

> [15] *"But the priests ... the sons of Zadok, <u>who kept charge of My sanctuary</u> when the children of Israel went astray from Me, they shall <u>come near Me</u> to minister to Me."* *(Ezek. 44:15)*

B. *We Minister to God*
We minister to God by declaring His supremacy, worth, beauty, and riches with adoration and gratitude. We minister to, glorify, and magnify God when we discern and delight in His beauty by treasuring, enjoying, celebrating, and making much of His name and beauty and by declaring it to others and reflecting it in our lives. As we praise or verbalize what we see of God's beauty, our insight and delight increase and our hearts are realigned to it.

C. *We Labor in Intercession*
We labor in intercession to release a greater measure of God's power to win the lost, revive the Church, and impact society while also engaging in works of justice and compassion. Constant intercession changes the spiritual atmosphere of the region in which the gospel is proclaimed, and the work of the kingdom goes forth in a greater release of power for healing, salvation, and justice.

D. *We Grow in Intimacy with God*
We grow in intimacy with God by personally encountering Him by the indwelling Spirit. We receive greater grace to love, obey, and partner with Him as we are fascinated by who He is and as we see the majestic beauty of God as Father and of Jesus as the Bridegroom, King, and Judge.

E. *We Grow in Understanding of the Word*

We grow in revelation of the Word, gaining insight into God's will, ways, and salvation, and as forerunners seeking to understand the unique dynamics of His end-time plan (Dan. 11:33). We serve others in an important way by spending time and effort to grow in our understanding of the Word, that we may help others understand God's heart and will for this hour of history.

F. *We Resource Other Prayer Ministries*

We resource many prayer ministries across the nations by providing our 24/7 prayer room web stream to provide live worship teams for them.

II. How to Engage in the Prayer Room

A. **Speak Words to God:** Sing the words of worship songs or repeat the prayers prayed on the mic.

B. **Bible Study Plan:** If you read ten chapters of the NT per day (six days a week) you will read through the NT once a month. Study for your IHOPU classes; study handouts or notes from FC, EGS, CBETS or your worship team Bible studies, etc.

C. **Pray in the Spirit:** Pray in the spirit, focusing on God's throne (Rev. 4–5). We edify our spirit and receive mysteries or revelation from God by this (1 Cor. 14:2, 4). Paul prayed in the spirit more than all others (1 Cor. 14:18).

D. **Personal Prayer List:** Pray to receive strength in your inner man (Eph. 3:16). See the F-E-L-L-O-W-S-H-I-P prayer in *Prayers to Strengthen Your Inner Man* for ten prayers for your *heart* (love, fear of God, purity) and your *mind* (spirit of revelation) and our *ministry* (increase of God's power to impact the lives of others).

E. **Prayer List for Others:** Praying for others includes praying for revival for a specific city, specific areas of justice in the government, and specific people (friends, ministries, unsaved, sick, etc.).

III. IHOPKC's Primary Calling and Five Specific Ministry Assignments

A. **The Primary Calling** for every ministry is to know God and to make Him known, as they work together with others to build the Church and engage in the Great Commission. This includes proclaiming the supremacy of Jesus as we win the lost, make disciples, heal the sick, build godly families, do works of justice and compassion, and seek to impact each sphere of society. We spread the fame of Jesus, proclaiming the knowledge of God and the worth of His Son.

19"Go … make disciples of all the nations … 20 teaching them to observe all things that I have commanded you." (Mt. 28:19–20)

18"I will build My church, and the gates of Hades shall not prevail against it." (Mt. 16:18)

B. The Lord gives most individuals and ministries specific assignments within the general, biblical mandate to build the Church and engage in the Great Commission.

C. **Our Five Specific Ministry Assignments**

1. **To keep a 24/7 sanctuary of worship with intercession** in the spirit of the tabernacle of David (1 Chr. 16:4–6, 37–42; Ezek. 44:15). The spiritual atmosphere of cities is changed through 24/7 prayer. We are contending for a greater breakthrough of God's power on the Church and society that results in renewing the Church, winning the lost, healing the sick, and releasing justice in society.

2. **To call people to walk out the first commandment, empowered by seeing Jesus as their Bridegroom King**. Grace-based holiness flows from intimacy with God and is expressed by seeking to obey Jesus by walking out the Sermon on the Mount lifestyle (Mt. 5–7).

3. **To proclaim the forerunner message**—Jesus as Bridegroom, King, and Judge; to prepare ourselves and others spiritually for the unique dynamics of God's endtime plan.

4. **To work with others to serve God's purposes for Israel**, including a 24/7, virtual, worldwide prayer network that seeks to mobilize 100 million intercessors.

5. **To strengthen the praying Church**, which includes developing resources and helping others to start houses of prayer (which are independent and not under IHOPKC) and to establish a culture of prayer in the Church in every nation.

IV. The Benefits of Night-and-Day Prayer

A. ***To glorify Jesus:*** providing a place to minister to God as we offer Him the praise of which He is worthy

B. ***For spiritual warfare:*** providing a place to change the spiritual atmosphere of a region

C. ***For personal transformation:*** providing a place of encounter and fascination with God

D. ***For training in the Word:*** providing a place to sing the Word, creating a singing seminary

E. ***For healing:*** providing a place where God's power heals the sick and tormented in body and soul

F. ***For unity:*** providing a place of reconciliation, where hearts are tenderized and pre-occupied with God (Ps. 133)

G. ***For direction:*** providing a place in which to receive fresh directives and understanding from the Lord

6

JESUS, THE BRIDEGROOM KING

Revelation 22:17 is one of the most informative and significant biblical prophecies, describing the end-time church as being in unity with what the Spirit is saying and doing in the generation of the Lord's return.

> *¹⁷ **The Spirit and the bride** say, "Come!" And let him who hears say, "Come!" And let him who thirsts come … ²⁰ "I am coming quickly." Amen. Even so, come, Lord Jesus! (Rev. 22:17, 20)*

This prophecy describes the Church in deep unity with the Holy Spirit, saying and doing what the Holy Spirit is saying and doing. What is the Spirit saying? He is speaking to believers about their identity as a Bride. What is the Spirit doing? He is interceding for Jesus to come to His Church in power, and He is calling thirsty people to come to Jesus as the Bridegroom God. John depicts the Church calling out in both these ways.

In this prophecy, John describes the highest function of the Church in four ways:

1. *Empowered* by the Spirit
2. *Engaged* in intercession
3. *Established* in her bridal identity
4. *Effective* in the harvest

In the end times, for the first time in history, the Spirit will universally emphasize the Church's identity as Jesus' Bride. It is not the Spirit and the *family* who will say, "Come," nor the Spirit and the army, kingdom, body, temple, or priesthood, though we will rejoice in those aspects of our identity forever. Rather, it is the Spirit resting on the Church as a *Bride*. For the first time in history, the Church worldwide will be in dynamic unity with the Spirit. Therefore, the Spirit will be resting on and moving through the Church in great power.

The Bridegroom message is focused on Jesus' *emotions* for us, His *beauty*, His *commitments* to us (to share His heart, home, throne, secrets, and beauty), and *our response* of wholehearted love (obedience) that moves Him. It begins with experiencing Jesus' affections and His desire for us. Jesus delights in us and enjoys us; He values our work and partners with us in it; He cares about our welfare and is committed to our eternal success.

Jesus is the Bridegroom King. He is the *King with power* and the *Bridegroom with desire*. Many are accustomed to Jesus the King who has power to rule over us, but they are not so familiar with Jesus the Bridegroom who desires to relate to us with overflowing love. Jesus is looking for relationship, not just a workforce. (Note: in no sense are there any sensual overtones in understanding Jesus as our Bridegroom.)

The Bridegroom message is a call to intimacy with God—to experience the deep things of His heart—His emotions, desires, and affections for us and His thoughts about us.

As sons of God, we are positioned to experience *God's throne* as heirs of His power and authority (Rev. 3:21; cf. Rom. 8:17). As Jesus' Bride, we are positioned to experience *God's heart* (emotions, affections, etc.). Just as women are the sons of God, so men are the Bride of Christ. Both describe our unique position of privilege before God, rather than pointing to something that is intrinsically male or female. Most Christian women do not struggle with the idea of being sons of God, because they do not see it as a call to be less feminine. Men often struggle with being the Bride of Christ, because they wrongly conclude that it is a call to be less masculine.

Experiencing the reality of being the Bride of Christ does not undermine a man's masculinity; rather it strengthens and establishes his manhood. When we come to understand Jesus as a passionate Bridegroom, we will soon see ourselves as His cherished Bride. Intimacy causes our hearts to be lovesick for Jesus—set on fire, enraptured, overcome by His love.

7

THE END-TIME PRAYER MOVEMENT

There is a significant relationship between the end-time worship and prayer movement and the revelation of Jesus as our Bridegroom God. Some stumble over this truth, but it is essential that we emphasize the revelation that His eternal nature is all-consuming love (1 Jn. 4:16).

Worship and prayer change the spiritual atmosphere of the region in focus as demons are driven back, angels are more active, and the Spirit moves in a greater measure (Dan. 10:12-13, 20–21). This causes the preaching of the gospel and the works of the kingdom to have a greater impact.

Before Jesus returns, the Spirit will raise up the greatest prayer movement in history. There are many indicators of this in Scripture (Ps. 96:1, 9, 13; 98:1–9; 102:15–22; 122:6; 149:6–9; Isa. 19:20–22; 24:14–16, 23; 25:9; 26:1, 8–9; 27:2–5, 13; 30:18–19, 29, 32; 35:2, 10; 42:10–15; 43:26; 51:11; 52:8; 62:6–7; Jer. 31:7; 51:8; Joel 2:12–17, 32; Zeph. 2:1–3; Zech. 8:20–23; 10:1; 12:10; 13:9; Mt. 21:13; 25:1–13; Lk. 18:7–8; Rev. 5:8; 6:9–11; 8:3–5; 9:13; 14:18; 16:7; 18:6; 22:17).

Psalms 96 and 98 both prophesy of a time when singing to the Lord will arise from all the earth.

> ¹*Sing to the LORD, <u>all the earth</u> ... ⁹worship the LORD ... Tremble before Him, <u>all the earth</u>. (Ps. 96:1, 9)*

> ³*<u>All the ends of the earth</u> have seen the salvation of our God ⁴... <u>all the earth</u>; break forth in song. (Ps. 98:3–4)*

May the Lord establish 24/7 prayer with worship in every tribe and tongue on earth before Jesus returns! This may happen across a region (not usually in one building) as many ministries work together in population centers.

The eternal identity of the redeemed is to be a *house of prayer*. The essence of prayer is that God speaks and moves our heart, and then we speak and move His heart, so that He releases His resources on earth.

> ⁶ *"The sons of the <u>foreigner</u> [Gentiles] who join themselves to the LORD, to ... love the name of the LORD ... ⁷ I will ... make them joyful in My house ... My house shall be <u>called a house of prayer for all nations</u>." (Isa. 56:6–7)*

When God names someone, it indicates how they function in the Spirit. Even "foreigners" who love Jesus—Gentile believers—are to experience enjoyable prayer (Isa. 56:7).

The Lord desires to be worshiped on earth as He is in heaven (Mt. 6:10).

In Revelation 4–5, John described the worship order established after God's own heart; it reveals how He wants to be worshiped. The heavenly order of worship is *continual, musical,* and *God-centered* (Rev. 4:8; 5:8–9; 14:2; 15:2). God-centered worship focuses on God and His personality and actions.

> *⁸The four living creatures … do not rest <u>day or night</u>, saying: "Holy, holy, holy, Lord God …"* (Rev. 4:8)
>
> *⁸ The twenty-four elders … each having a <u>harp</u> … ⁹ sang a new song. (Rev. 5:8–9)*

Isaiah and the End-Time Prayer Movement

Isaiah wrote more on the earthly dimension of the end-time worship movement than any man in the Bible, whereas the book of Revelation gives the most information on the heavenly dimension of the prayer movement.

Isaiah prophesied concerning singing before the Bridegroom God (Isa. 54:4–12; 62:2–5):

> *¹ "Sing, O barren, you who have not borne! Break forth into singing, and cry aloud … ⁵ For <u>your Maker is your husband</u>, the LORD of hosts is His name." (Isa. 54:1, 5)*

Israel was accustomed to God being the transcendent King with power, but not the Bridegroom with desire. Singing to the Bridegroom God is singing that reveals and imparts love.

Isaiah prophesied that the end-time prayer movement would be:

Relational, encountering a Bridegroom God (Isa. 54:5; 62:5)

Musical (Isa. 24:14–16; 26:1; 27:2; 30:29, 32; 35:2, 10; 42:10–12; 54:1)

Continual (Isa. 62:6–7)

Global (Isa. 24:16; 42:10–12)

Missional (Isa. 54:13–14; 62:6–12)

Isaiah connected the revelation of Jesus as Bridegroom to the end-time prayer movement continuing 24/7 (Isa. 62:4–7). The Spirit will establish a worldwide wall of intercession that will not stop until Jerusalem becomes "a praise in the earth" at the time of Jesus' return. The bridal revelation of Isaiah 62:3–5 is essential to sustaining the night-and-day prayer of verses 6 and 7.

> *⁴ You shall be called Hephzibah … for the Lord delights in you … ⁵ as the <u>bridegroom rejoices over the bride</u>, so shall your God rejoice over you. ⁶ I have set watchmen [intercessors] on your walls, O Jerusalem; <u>they shall never hold their peace day or night</u> … ⁷ give Him no rest till He establishes and till He makes Jerusalem a praise in the earth. (Isa. 62:4–7)*

Isaiah prophesied about the end-time worship movement throughout Isaiah 24–27. He saw the defeat of God's enemies and the return of Jesus (24:21–23) in connection with the worship movement (24:14–16), which focuses on the majesty and beauty of Jesus (24:14).

> *¹⁴ They shall lift up their voice, <u>they shall sing</u>; for the <u>majesty of the Lord</u> … ¹⁵ glorify the Lord in the dawning light, the name of the Lord God of Israel in the coastlands of the sea. ¹⁶ From the <u>ends of the earth</u> we have heard songs: "Glory to the righteous!" (Isa. 24:14–16)*

In Isaiah 42, Isaiah prophesied about a global intercessory worship movement (42:10–12), which would usher in Jesus' return (42:13) and release His end-time judgments (42:14–15).

> *¹⁰ <u>Sing to the Lord a new song</u>, and His praise <u>from the ends of the earth</u>, you who go down to the sea, and all that is in it, you coastlands … ¹¹ Let the wilderness and its cities lift up their voice, the villages that Kedar inhabits. Let the inhabitants of Sela sing, let them shout from the top of the mountains … ¹³ The Lord <u>shall go forth</u> [Jesus' second coming] like a mighty man; He shall stir up His zeal like a man of war. He shall cry out, yes, shout aloud; He shall prevail against His enemies … ¹⁵ "I will lay waste the mountains [earthquakes]." (Isa. 42:10–15)*

The Spirit is calling His people to work together to offer continual intercession in each city, flowing from prophetic worship (music) and intimacy with God, to fulfill the Great Commission—to win and disciple the lost, to revive the Church, and to impact society with the love, power, and wisdom of God.

In summary, the end-time prayer movement engages in prayer *for the harvest, with music*, and *from intimacy* with God. It is more than prayer for personal circumstances—for direction, protection, provision, healing, and so on, which are valid prayers. When we pray for the harvest among the nations and for missions, we are asking for a breakthrough of the power of the gospel in a city, nation, or specific region.

8

THE LEVITES—THE FULL-TIME OCCUPATION
OF SINGERS AND MUSICIANS

I.   Understanding God's Will—Your Calling and Ministry Assignment

The highest calling we can have is the one that God gives us in the various seasons of our life. My desire is that everyone on GPR teams walks in God's will for their life with clarity related to God's calling on their life. It is helpful to know *what* you are doing and *why* you are doing it.

> *⁹ We ... ask that you may be <u>filled with the knowledge of His will in all wisdom</u> ... ¹⁰ that you may walk <u>worthy</u> of the Lord, fully <u>pleasing</u> Him, being fruitful in every good work. (Col. 1:9–10)*

We ask our staff members to function as intercessory missionaries during their time at IHOPKC and to uphold and honor our vision, values, and messaging and participate in our family life together. For some this is your *long-term calling* and for others it is a *short-term ministry assignment*.

II.   Worship on Earth as It Is in Heaven

The Lord desires to be worshiped on earth as He is in heaven. In Revelation 4–5, John described aspects of the worship order that were established after God's own heart—the heavenly worship order is *continual, musical, relational,* and *God-centered* (Rev. 4:8; 5:8–9; 15:2).

The Lord revealed many things to David about how He desires to be worshiped, giving David insight into a new worship order that He wanted established on the earth.

> *¹¹ David gave his son Solomon the plans ... ¹² for all that he had by the Spirit, of the courts of the house of the LORD ... ¹³ also for the division of the priests and the Levites, <u>for all the work of the service of the house of the LORD</u> ... ¹⁹ "All this," said David, "the LORD made me understand in writing, <u>by His hand upon me</u>, all the works of these plans." (1 Chr. 28:11–19)*

The Lord revealed to David a new order for worship and commanded him to command the kings of Israel after him to establish it (1 Chr. 28:11–19; cf. 2 Chr. 29:25; 35:4, 15; Ezra 3:10; Neh. 12:45). This included establishing a full-time occupation for singers and musicians to minister to the Lord.

> *²⁵ [Hezekiah] <u>stationed the Levites</u> in the house of the LORD with cymbals, with stringed instruments ... <u>according to the commandment of David</u> ... for thus was the <u>commandment of the LORD</u>. (2 Chr. 29:25)*

David set Levites in place to worship God before the ark. They received a *salary* and engaged in *daily service*. He established 4,000 paid musicians and singers together with 4,000 gatekeepers (1 Chr. 23:5; 25:7). He financed over 8,000 "staff" to facilitate worship. Israel was commanded to support the singers/musicians in the temple as their *full-time occupation* (1 Chr. 9:33; 16:37; 23:5; 25:7; 2 Chr. 8:12–14; 31:4–6, 16; 2 Chr. 34:9, 12; Neh. 10:37–39; 11:22–23; 12:44–47; 13:5–12).

> [33] *The singers ... were* <u>free from other duties;</u> *for they were* <u>employed in that work</u> *day and night.* (1 Chr. 9:33)

> [4] *He appointed some of the Levites [singers and musicians] to minister before the ark ... to praise the LORD ...* [37] *He left Asaph and his brothers there ... to minister before the ark regularly,* <u>as every day's work required.</u> (1 Chr. 16:4, 37)

> [14] *According to the order of David his father, he [Solomon] appointed ... Levites* <u>for their duties</u> *(to praise ...)* <u>as the duty of each day required</u> *... for so David ... commanded. (2 Chr. 8:14)*

> [16] *They distributed to everyone ... his* <u>daily portion</u> *for the* <u>work of his service</u>*. (2 Chr. 31:16)*

What did it look like for the Levites to do this as an occupation for nearly 1,000 years during the Old Testament period? They received a salary and an honored position in Israel's society. But they had no electricity, air conditioning, running water, recording studios, or emails to find replacements. It was their real occupation and sacred trust. They had no concerts or CDs. They had no opportunities outside of the sanctuary. They did it as before God's eyes; it was not a stepping-stone to their future music career.

When Israel went astray, God raised up reformers with a vision to restore worship as David commanded. Each of the seven periods of "revivals" after David embraced full-time singers and musicians. *Solomon* began his reign around 970 BC; he embraced the occupation of full-time singers and musicians (2 Chr. 8:14). *Jehoshaphat's* reform began around 870 BC; it included the full-time occupation of singers and musicians (2 Chr. 20:21, 28). Around 835 BC, *Jehoiada* restored temple worship in the order of David (2 Chr. 23:18). *Hezekiah's* revival began around 725 BC; it included restoring singers and musicians (2 Chr. 29:25). *Josiah's* revival began around 625 BC; he restored full-time singers and musicians (2 Chr. 35:3–15). In about 536 BC, *Zerubbabel* established full-time singers and musicians (Ezra 3:10), as did *Ezra* and *Nehemiah* in 445 BC (Neh. 12:24, 45).

God commanded Israel to support the singers financially (2 Kgs. 22:3–7; 1 Chr. 9:33; 16:37; 2 Chr. 8:14; 31:4-16; 34:9–13; Neh. 11:22–23; 12:44–47). I believe that the Lord will again speak strongly to His people to support singers, musicians, intercessors, and "gatekeepers" financially.

> ⁵ *The tithes … were <u>commanded</u> to be given to the … singers …* ¹⁰ *I also realized that the portions for the Levites had not been given them; for each of the … singers who did the work <u>had gone back to his field</u>.* ¹¹ *So I <u>contended with the rulers</u>, and said, "Why is the house of God forsaken?" And I gathered them together and <u>set them in their place</u>.* ¹² *Then <u>all Judah brought the tithe</u> … to the storehouse. (Neh. 13:5–12)*

The Spirit is raising up the most powerful worship movement in history (Lk. 18:7–8; Rev. 5:8; 8:4; 22:17; Isa. 24:14–16; 25:9; 26:8–9; 27:2–5, 13; 30:18–19; 42:10–13; 51:11; 52:8; 62:6–7; Jer. 31:7).

One principle essential to sustaining 24/7 prayer with worship is the full-time occupation of singers and musicians. There are both theological and practical reasons for this. The calling to be a full-time intercessory missionary is rooted in Scripture, church history, and end-time prophecy. (See the next chapter: *The Call to Be a Full-Time Intercessory Missionary*).

Practical: It is more difficult for teams to grow together musically, relationally, and spiritually without being together in a full-time way, making it more challenging to sustain a 24/7 sanctuary.

Embracing this full-time occupation only makes sense when we see it as a sacred calling that God *delights in* and *requires* for some. Seeing this as a privilege before God helps us to manage the many challenges associated with it. Some are on IHOPKC worship teams for a season of training or as a stepping-stone to their future ministry—that is good. Their work is greatly appreciated. But for those who see it as an opportunity to open doors for future ministry, there are pitfalls to beware of.

Application: All who join a GPR worship team should be in *pursuit* of doing it as a full-time occupation. There are exceptions for *moms* who were previously on staff (if they are willing to be on four sets a week—I see this as heroic dedication) and for IHOPU *students* on worship teams.

III. The Worship Order Established by King David

1. David commanded God's people to honor the heavenly order of worship that he received by revelation because it was God's command (2 Chr. 29:25; 35:4, 15; Ezra 3:10; Neh. 12:45).

   25 [Hezekiah] stationed Levites in the house of the LORD with … stringed instruments … according to the commandment of David … for thus was the commandment of the LORD. (2 Chr. 29:25)

2. David put Levites before the ark of the covenant (which spoke of God's throne) to worship God.

   1 They brought the ark of God, and set it in the midst of the <u>tabernacle that David</u> had erected for it … 4 He appointed some of the Levites [singers] to minister before the ark … to praise the LORD … 37 to minister before the ark regularly, <u>as every day's work required</u>. (1 Chr. 16:1, 4, 37)

3. David established 4,000 paid musicians, 288 singers (12 x 24 = 288), and 4,000 gatekeepers. Thus, he financed about 10,000 full-time staff to facilitate worship.

   7 The number … instructed in the songs of the LORD … who were skillful, <u>was two hundred and eighty-eight</u>. (1 Chr. 25:7)

   5 Four thousand were gatekeepers, and <u>four thousand praised the LORD with musical instruments</u>. (1 Chr. 23:5)

4. David provided financial support so that singers could sing as a full-time occupation.

   33 These are the singers … who lodged in the chambers, and were <u>free from other duties;</u> for they were <u>employed in that work</u> day and night. (1 Chr. 9:33)

5. God's order for supporting the singers and gatekeepers was revealed to David.

   37 So he left Asaph and his brothers there before the ark of the covenant of the LORD to minister before the ark <u>regularly</u>, as <u>every day's work required</u>. (1 Chr. 16:37)

6. David gave over $100 billion (at modern prices) to God's house. One talent is 75 pounds or 1,200 ounces (16 oz./lb.) and would be worth about 1 million dollars ($800/oz.). Thus, 100,000 talents of gold is worth about $100 billion; a talent of silver ($12/oz.) is worth about $15,000.

   14 I have taken <u>much trouble</u> to prepare for the house of the LORD one hundred thousand talents of gold [about $100 billion] and one million talents of silver [about $15 billion]. (1 Chr. 22:14)

7. Amos (about 750 BC) prophesied of the restoration of David's tabernacle. The fullness of the tabernacle of David speaks of Jesus' millennial government based on 24/7 Davidic worship.

> *¹¹ "On that day <u>I will raise up the tabernacle of David</u>, which has fallen down, and repair its damages; I will raise up its ruins, and rebuild it <u>as in the days of old.</u>" (Amos 9:11)*

8. When Israel went astray, God raised up spiritual reformers with a vision to restore worship as David commanded it. All of the seven "revivals" in Old Testament times restored Davidic worship.

9. Solomon established singers (about 970 BC) according to the command that God gave David.

> *¹⁴ <u>According to the order of David his father</u>, he [Solomon] appointed … Levites for their duties (to praise …) as the duty of each day required … for so David … commanded. (2 Chr. 8:14)*

10. Jehoshaphat's reform (about 870 BC) included establishing singers and musicians.

> *¹⁹ The Levites … stood up to praise the L<small>ORD</small> … ²¹ <u>He appointed those who should sing to the L<small>ORD</small></u> … ²⁸ They came … <u>with stringed instruments</u> … to the house of the L<small>ORD</small>. (2 Chr. 20:19–28)*

11. Jehoiada the high priest restored temple worship in the order of David (about 835 BC) with singers and musicians and enthroned King Jehoash (Joash) when he was only seven years old.

> *¹⁶ Jehoiada [high priest] made a covenant between himself, the people, and the king, that they should be the L<small>ORD</small>'s people … ¹⁸ Jehoiada <u>appointed</u> the oversight of the house of the L<small>ORD</small> to … <u>the Levites … with singing, as it was established by David</u>. (2 Chr. 23:16, 18)*

12. Hezekiah's revival (about 725 BC) included restoring singers/musicians as David commanded.

> *²⁵He stationed the Levites in the house of the L<small>ORD</small> with … stringed instruments … <u>according to the commandment of David</u> … ²⁷ The song of the L<small>ORD</small> also began … (2 Chr. 29:25, 27)*

13. Josiah's revival (about 625 BC) restored full-time singers and musicians as David commanded.

> *³ He said to the Levites … ⁴ "Prepare yourselves … <u>following the written instruction of David</u> …" ¹⁵ The singers … were in their places, <u>according to the command of David</u>. (2 Chr. 35:3–15)*

14. Zerubbabel (about 536 BC) established full-time singers and musicians as commanded by David.

   ¹⁰ The Levites ... to praise the Lord, <u>according to the ordinance of David</u>. (Ezra 3:10)

   ⁴⁷ In the days of Zerubbabel and in the days of Nehemiah all Israel gave the portions for the singers and the gatekeepers, a portion for each day. (Neh. 12:47)

15. Ezra and Nehemiah (445 BC) established full-time singers and musicians as David commanded.

   ²⁴ The Levites ... give thanks ... <u>according to the command of David</u> ... ⁴⁵ The singers and the gatekeepers kept the charge of their God ... according to the command of David. (Neh. 12:24, 45)

God's desire to be worshiped on earth as He is in heaven has not changed (Mt. 6:10). The Spirit has not emphasized this through history, but now is in many nations. The order of worship that God commanded David to embrace is timeless, such as establishing singers and musicians in God's house. The application will differ in each culture. Isaiah 42 declares this will happen before Jesus' return.

   ¹⁰ Sing to the Lord a <u>new song</u>, and His praise from the ends of the earth, <u>you who go down to the sea</u> ... you <u>coastlands</u> ... ¹¹ Let the <u>wilderness</u> and its cities lift up their voice, the <u>villages</u> that Kedar [Saudi Arabia] inhabits. Let the <u>inhabitants of Sela</u> [Jordan] sing ... ¹³ The <u>Lord shall go forth like a mighty man</u> [Jesus' second coming]; He shall stir up His zeal like a man of war. He shall cry out, yes, shout aloud; He shall prevail against His enemies." (Isa. 42:10–13)

9

THE CALL TO BE A FULL-TIME INTERCESSORY MISSIONARY

I.   What Is an Intercessory Missionary?

As the Holy Spirit highlights the call to prayer in this generation, He is calling some to take up a full-time ministry occupation that I refer to as an *"intercessory missionary."* Sometimes I am asked what an intercessory missionary is and where this ministry is found in the Bible. We do not find the specific title of "intercessory missionary" used in the Bible, but neither do we find ministry titles of senior pastor, marriage counselor, youth pastor, children's pastor, or outreach pastor. The Bible does not give a comprehensive list of the titles of ministries that the Spirit has used throughout church history. I believe the Body of Christ has liberty to use different ministry titles and focuses, as long as they represent biblical values being upheld.

We see that the essence of the calling and occupation of an intercessory missionary is found throughout the Bible. *I define an intercessory missionary as one whose full-time occupation is to do the work of the kingdom from the place of prayer and worship while embracing a missionary lifestyle and focus.* Others may define this term in a different way. At IHOPKC, as a rule, we ask those who embrace this full-time occupation of intercessory missionary to serve fifty hours per week—this includes being in the prayer room several hours a day along with being engaged in service and/or ministry to others.

We will look at this calling in the Old Testament and the New Testament—particularly in end-time prophecy—its presence throughout church history, and how it is being embraced today in contemporary ministries.

II.   The Value of Night-and-Day Prayer in Heaven

Revelation 4–5 describes the worship order around God's throne. Those nearest the throne magnify Him and agree with His purposes through their constant worship and intercession. The worthiness of God demands 24/7 worship, and this value will be embraced and expressed forever.

> [8] *The four living creatures … do not rest day or night, saying: "Holy, holy, holy, Lord God …"* (*Rev. 4:8*)

Jesus exhorted us to pray that His will be done *on earth as it is in heaven* (Mt. 6:10). One aspect of God's kingdom being expressed on earth as it is in heaven involves worship. God's desire to be worshiped on earth as He is in heaven has not changed. The Holy Spirit has not emphasized this globally through history, but is now emphasizing it to believers in many nations. The value of the worship around the throne is timeless; its applications on earth have differed in each generation and culture.

III.   Intercessory Missionaries in End-Time Prophecy

The Holy Spirit will establish the most powerful prayer and worship movement in history at the end of the age. The Scriptures indicate the significance of prayer in the end times (Lk. 18:7–8; Rev. 5:8; 8:4; 22:17; cf. Isa. 24:14–16; 25:9; 26:8–9; 27:13; 30:18–19; 42:10–13; 43:26; 52:8; 62:6–7; Jer. 31:7). Prayer is one of the major themes of end-time prophecy. The conflict at the end of the age will be between two global worship movements. The Antichrist will empower a worldwide, state-financed, false-worship movement (Rev. 13:4, 8, 12, 15), but the global prayer movement led by Jesus will be far more powerful.

Isaiah prophesied concerning prayer ministries that would continue 24/7 until Jesus returns—this is when Jesus will restore Jerusalem as a praise in the earth. Isaiah was speaking of the watchmen-intercessors the Lord Himself would appoint and set in place, who would not keep silent day or night.

> [6] *On your walls, O Jerusalem, I have appointed watchmen [intercessors]; all day and all night they will never keep silent. You who remind the LORD, take no rest for yourselves;* [7] *and give Him no rest until He establishes and makes Jerusalem a praise in the earth. (Isa. 62:6–7 NASB)*

We know that this promise has a particular reference to the end times because it refers to God-ordained 24/7 prayer ministries that will *never be silent until Jerusalem becomes a praise in the earth*, which happens in the context of Jesus' second coming. Many prayer ministries have been initiated by the Lord throughout history, but they ended after a season. But Isaiah spoke of a particular category of prayer ministries *that never stop until Jesus' return*. Many such new 24/7 prayer ministries have started across the earth in the last few decades.

The 24/7 dimension of this promise implies that some intercessors and ministries are called to engage in this as a full-time occupation. God's promise to appoint intercessors implies that He will make a way for them to walk in this calling, which would include financial provision. Some whom He appoints will be *full-time occupational intercessors*. Their hard work in prayer and worship will inevitably serve and strengthen other prayer ministries in churches in their region and will be catalytic by inspiring and supporting others in prayer.

Only one generation will see the fulfillment of God's promise to appoint, or set, watchmen (intercessors) in place to cry out all day and all night *until* Jerusalem becomes a praise in the earth. This prophecy speaks specifically of prayer ministries being established by the Lord that will continue *until* He returns, for Jerusalem will become a praise in the earth only after Jesus returns. At that time, all the nations will see Jerusalem as Jesus' own city, as the city of the Great King (Ps. 48:2; Jer. 3:17; Mt. 5:35).

Isaiah's prophecy speaks of a spiritual wall of intercession from which the *end-time* watchmen/intercessors will cry out 24/7 for the release of God's promises. Ezekiel also spoke of spiritual walls consisting of prayer (Ezek. 13:3–5; 22:30). God will establish end-time intercessors in their place on the "wall of prayer." These watchmen are to make the wall by standing in the gap in prayer before God and the people, so that the land may be blessed rather than destroyed.

The gravity of this promise: Through Isaiah, God made a sovereign promise to appoint intercessors and establish them in the work of intercession that will never stop *until* Jesus returns. This will include full-time occupational intercessors who will stand on the wall of intercession to cry out for God's purposes for Jerusalem.

IV. Intercessory Missionaries in the New Testament

I remind you that I used the term *intercessory missionary* to speak of one whose full-time occupation is to do the work of the kingdom from the place of prayer and worship while embracing a missionary lifestyle and focus. Some ask where the lifestyle of an intercessory missionary is found in the New Testament. I reply by asking a different question: where in the New Testament do we find leaders who do *not* prioritize prayer? Starting with Jesus and the apostles, the New Testament highlights many leaders who gave themselves to prayer in an extravagant way.

As we have seen, Jesus spent long hours in prayer (Mk. 1:35; 6:46; Lk. 5:16; 6:12; 9:18, 28).

Jesus valued Mary of Bethany's choice to sit before Him; He called it the one thing needed (Lk. 10:38–42). He emphasized prayer, or "watching," more than any other specific activity when speaking about the generation in which He would return (Mt. 24:42–43; 25:13; Mk. 13:33–37; Lk. 21:36; Rev. 3:3; 16:15). Watch: (Mt. 24:42–43; 25:13; 26:38–41; 27:36; Mk. 13:33–38; Lk. 12:38–39; 21:36; Acts 20:31; 1 Cor. 16:13; 1 Thes. 5:2–4, 6; Rev. 3:3; 16:15).

Paul embraced elements of night-and-day prayer in various seasons and even called widows to this ministry (1 Thes. 3:10; 1 Tim. 5:5; 2 Tim. 1:3).

John the Baptist spent a lot of time communing with the Lord in the wilderness of Judea (Mt. 3).

The apostles were committed to their prayer lives (Acts 6:4).

Cornelius was a centurion by occupation, yet he is called a man who "prayed to God always" (Acts 10:2), and an angel said that his continual prayers were a memorial before God (Acts 10:4).

Prayer was a high priority for the leaders in the New Testament (see Acts 1:14, 24; 2:42; 3:1; 4:31; 6:4; 9:11; 10:2, 9, 30–31; 11:5; 12:5, 12; 13:3; 14:23; 16:16, 25; Rom. 8:26; 10:1; 12:12; 1 Cor. 7:5; 2 Cor. 1:11; 9:14; 13:7–9; Eph. 1:17–19; 3:14–21; 6:18; Phil. 1:4, 9–11; 4:6; Col. 1:3, 9–11; 4:2–3; 1 Thes. 3:10; 5:17, 25; 2 Thes. 1:11; 3:1; 1 Tim. 2:8; 4:5; Heb. 13:18; Jas. 5:13–18; Jude 20).

Consider just a few of the many statements reflecting the value of prayer in the New Testament:

> ⁴² *They __continued steadfastly__ in the apostles' doctrine and fellowship … and in __prayers__. (Acts 2:42)*

> ⁴ *"We will give ourselves __continually to prayer__ and to the ministry of the word." (Acts 6:4)*

> ¹⁰ *… night and day __praying exceedingly__ that we may … perfect what is lacking in your faith? (1 Thes. 3:10)*

> ¹⁷ *__Pray without ceasing__; ¹⁸ … for this is the will of God in Christ Jesus for you. (1 Thes. 5:17–18)*

It is easy to find leaders in the New Testament who were consistently engaging in prayer and the Word; it is actually difficult to find a precedent for leaders who did not do this. God's kingdom work is accomplished in the place of prayer and outside of it: three dimensions of missions work—continual prayer, mercy deeds, and sharing the gospel—must go together. Prayer causes the work of outreach to the lost and needy to be much more effective. Oswald Chambers said, "Prayer does not fit us for the greater work; prayer *is* the greater work." (*My Utmost for His Highest*, "Greater Works.")

Some are concerned that intercessory missionaries may develop lazy, isolated lives in prayer, detached from the real needs of people. Anyone who has prayed four hours in one day, with fasting, and then gone out to preach the gospel, will know that the call to be an intercessory missionary is not for lazy people. Some ask if too much prayer leads intercessors to neglect walking in love for others. I have observed just the opposite.

Night-and-day prayer is a practical expression of the commandment to love one another, through which multitudes are blessed and delivered. Indeed, intercessors grow in love for the ones they take up in prayer. When someone has a family member who is being tormented by a demon, that family member needs someone to cast the demon out. Jesus linked greater effectiveness in casting out demons to prayer and fasting. He spoke of the need for prayer and fasting when ministering to certain kinds of demonized people (Mt. 17:21). In other words, the rigorous lifestyle of an intercessory missionary is one that embraces the first and second commandments to love God and love others.

V.   The Anna Calling

Anna was a *watchman* set upon the wall in Jerusalem. We see an expression of Isaiah's prophecy in Anna, who prayed in the temple "night and day" (Isa. 62:6; Lk. 2:36–38). She was a token of what will happen across the nations during the generation in which the Lord returns.

> *36 Now there was one, Anna, a prophetess … She was of a great age, and had lived with a husband seven years from her virginity; 37 and this woman was a widow of about eighty-four years, who did not depart from the temple, but served God with fastings and prayers night and day. 38 … she gave thanks to the Lord, and spoke of Him [Jesus] to all those who looked for redemption in Jerusalem. (Lk. 2:36–38)*

Notice that Anna was a prophetess (v. 36), intercessor (v. 37), and evangelist (v. 38). The grace for prophetic ministry, intercession, and evangelism came together in one woman. Anna was widowed after living with her husband for seven years (v. 36), probably when she was in her mid-twenties, and that is when she began giving herself to prayer by night and by day. At eighty-four years old—approximately sixty years later—Anna was still ministering to the Lord in much prayer with fasting. She stayed faithful in her calling to long hours of prayer. What a remarkable woman!

Anna represents those with grace to sustain long hours of prayer for many years. Anna's calling transcends gender and age—this calling is for male and female, young and old. I refer to some intercessory missionaries as having a specific "Anna calling," by which I mean that they have grace for much prayer and fasting.

Anna is the most extreme example of the intercessory missionary lifestyle in the New Testament. She probably spent more hours in prayer each day than our intercessory missionaries do. In this very hour, the Lord is wooing those with a heart and calling like Anna to the full-time occupation of worship and prayer. He is personally appointing them and setting them in their places. The Lord is calling forth modern-day "Annas" in churches and prayer rooms around the world. We must celebrate those whom God raises up as Annas as a great gift to the Body of Christ and the prayer movement. These individuals need to be called forth, recognized, and released by their leaders to obey their God-given mandate.

Jesus made a reference to Isaiah's prophecy about night-and-day prayer when He promised that it would result in a great release of justice to the earth (Lk. 18:1–8).

> *⁷ "Will not God bring about justice for His elect who <u>cry to Him day and night</u> … ? ⁸ I tell you that He will bring about justice for them quickly. However, when the Son of Man comes [second coming], will He find faith on the earth?" (Lk. 18:7–8 NASB)*

In verse 8, Jesus connected the call to night-and-day prayer with the timing of His return to the earth. It is important to notice that this parable was given in conclusion to what He had just taught about the end times in Luke 17:22–36.

In other words, Jesus connected His release of justice in the earth during the end times to night-and-day prayer, and, in verse 8, He referred to the generation in which He will return.

VI. Intercessory Missionaries in the Old Testament

We find important information in the Old Testament about the full-time occupation of singers who ministered to God night and day. David commanded all the kings after him to uphold the order of worship that he had received from God, because it was God's command (2 Chr. 29:25; 35:4, 15; Ezra 3:10; Neh. 12:45).

> *²⁵ [Hezekiah] stationed the <u>Levites</u> in the house of the LORD with cymbals, with stringed instruments, and with harps, <u>according to the commandment of David</u> … thus was the <u>commandment of the LORD</u> by His prophets. (2 Chr. 29:25)*

David was the first one in Scripture to establish the full-time occupation of a worshiper (1 Chr. 9:33; 16:37; 23:5; 25:7; 2 Chr. 8:12–14; 31:4–6, 16; 34:9, 12; Neh. 10:37–39; 11:22–23; 12:44–47; 13:5–12).

> *³³ These are the <u>singers</u> … who lodged in the chambers, and were <u>free from other duties</u>; for they were <u>employed in that work day and night</u>. (1 Chr. 9:33)*

David established 4,000 musicians and 4,000 gatekeepers (1 Chr. 23:5; 25:7). Meaning, David set into place around 8,000 intercessory missionaries. They were Levites—some were singers and musicians, others were gatekeepers. (Today I would add sound technicians to this list, because, in my opinion, the sound board is an important instrument on a worship team.)

The gatekeepers took care of the buildings and finances and carried out many other activities to support the ministry to God in the temple. In our context, this speaks of those who help with finance or event management, janitorial or organizational service, running seminars, and so on.

The singers were employed in their work day and night, so they were freed from other duties. In other words, they did not have another job outside their temple responsibilities. Their job in the temple was hard work: they sang and played their instruments. I imagine they also had "worship team practices," had to grow in musical skill and knowledge of the Scripture, and many other related activities. God commanded David to establish this ministry of night-and-day worship. Though it required a significant amount of work and was very expensive, David insisted on making this costly investment of time and money, knowing that the Lord had commanded it and that the God of Israel is worthy of such praise.

When Israel went astray in the generations that followed David, God raised up spiritual reformers with a vision to restore worship as David had commanded. Seven generations in the Old Testament experienced revival. Each honored the command that God had given David, and restored Davidic worship, complete with full-time intercessory missionaries.

1. *King Solomon:* Around 970 BC, Solomon established the singers according to David's command (2 Chr. 8:14).

    ¹⁴ And, according to the order of David his father, he [Solomon] appointed the divisions of the priests for their service, the Levites for their duties (to praise and serve before the priests) as the duty of each day required ... for so David the man of God had commanded. (2 Chr. 8:14)

2. *King Jehoshaphat:* Around 870 BC, Jehoshaphat's reform included establishing singers and musicians.

    ¹⁹ Then the Levites ... stood up to praise the Lord ... ²¹ [Jehoshaphat] appointed those who should sing to the Lord ... as they went out before the army ... ²⁷ Then they returned ... for the Lord had made them rejoice over their enemies. ²⁸ So they came to Jerusalem, with stringed instruments ... to the house of the Lord. (2 Chr. 20:19–28)

3. *The high priest Jehoiada:* In about 835 BC, Jehoiada the high priest restored temple worship in the order of King David, with singers and musicians. The future King Jehoash (Joash) was only seven years old at the time.

    ¹⁸ Jehoiada appointed the oversight of the house of the Lord to ... the Levites ... with singing, as it was established by David. (2 Chr. 23:18)

4. *King Hezekiah:* Hezekiah's revival, around 725 BC, included restoring singers according to David's command.

   25 [Hezekiah] stationed the Levites in the house of the LORD with cymbals, with stringed instruments, and with harps, according to the commandment of David ... for thus was the commandment of the LORD by His prophets ... 27 And when the burnt offering began, the song of the LORD also began. (2 Chr. 29:25–27)

5. *King Josiah:* Around 625 BC, King Josiah restored full-time singers and musicians to their place, just as David had commanded the kings of Israel to do (2 Chr. 35:3–15).

   3 Then [Josiah] said to the Levites ... 4 "Prepare yourselves ... following the written instruction of David ..." 15 And the singers, the sons of Asaph, were in their places, according to the command of David. (2 Chr. 35:3–4, 15)

6. *Governor Zerubbabel:* Zerubbabel lived about 500 years after David, and during that time they were still putting singers in place because it was the command of David. Was this thing burning in God's heart? In 536 BC, Zerubbabel established full-time singers and musicians as a full-time occupation to worship God, because King David had commanded that this be done in Israel (Ezra 3:10–11; Neh. 12:47).

   10 When the builders laid the foundation of the temple of the LORD, the priests stood ... and the Levites ... to praise the LORD, according to the ordinance of David king of Israel. 11 And they sang responsively. (Ezra 3:10–11)

   45 Both the singers and the gatekeepers kept the charge of their God ... according to the command of David and Solomon his son. 46 For in the days of David and Asaph of old there were chiefs of the singers, and songs of praise and thanksgiving to God. 47 In the days of Zerubbabel and in the days of Nehemiah all Israel gave the portions [finances] for the singers and the gatekeepers, a portion for each day. (Neh. 12:45–47)

7. *Ezra and Nehemiah:* In 445 BC, Ezra and Nehemiah established full-time singers and musicians because King David had commanded it. Also at that time, God commanded Israel to support the singers financially in the same way that David had done (2 Chr. 8:14; 31:5–16; Neh. 11:23; 12:44–47; 13:5–12).

   24 And the heads of the Levites were ... to praise and give thanks, group alternating with group, according to the command of David ... 45 Both the singers and the gatekeepers kept the charge of their God ... according to the command of David ... 47 In the days of Zerubbabel and in the days of Nehemiah all Israel gave the portions [finances] for the singers and the gatekeepers, a portion for each day. (Neh. 12:24, 45–47)

VII. Intercessory Missionaries Throughout History

The Lord has led many throughout history to establish night-and-day prayer ministries. Looking back through church history, I see a golden thread of the Spirit testifying that this is on God's heart. Although it is clear that the Holy Spirit has not emphasized this calling to the whole Body of Christ through the 2,000 years of church history, He has clearly called some to this ministry. Thus, we see a witness of night-and-day prayer down the centuries, which is a testimony that God desires this kind of extravagant ministry from His people.

The order of worship that God commanded David to establish—full-time singers and musicians in God's house—is timeless and valid today, but the application of this command differs according to each generation and culture. Throughout 2,000 years of church history, intercessory missionaries have been known by different titles. However, we see the biblical values behind this occupation in that they did the work of missions from a lifestyle of being deeply engaged in prayer, worship, and the Word.

One of the most dramatic expressions of 24/7 intercessory prayer began with Comgall, a monk in Bangor, Ireland, in AD 558. After Comgall's death in AD 602, the annals reported that 3,000 monks had joined his monastery and maintained a 24/7 prayer ministry for over 300 years. It became an influential missions-sending community, famous for its choral psalmody and unceasing prayer.

In the past, most of the people who sustained 24/7 prayer ministries did so as their full-time occupation. Therefore, I refer to them as intercessory missionaries, although they themselves did not use that term. Most who embraced this calling in medieval times were monks, priests, or nuns, who lived in monastic communities.

Most monastic communities that sustained 24/7 prayer were involved in outreach to the cities nearby. Ministries from all streams of the Body of Christ have mobilized 24/7 prayer ministries, including Celtic, Orthodox, Catholic, and Protestant traditions.

1. *Alexander Akimetes*

   Around AD 380, Alexander established a monastery that maintained 24/7 worship and prayer. He organized rotating choirs into shifts to create uninterrupted prayer and worship twenty-four hours a day. He first organized this perpetual praise near the Euphrates River, where it lasted for twenty years. Then he and seventy monks moved to Constantinople in AD 400, where another 300 monks joined them to once again organize 24/7 prayer with praise, which lasted much longer this time as a movement. Since their prayer with praise never stopped, their group was referred to as "the order of the Acoemetae" (literally, the sleepless ones).

After Alexander's death in AD 430, the monastery's influence grew until, at the end of the fifth century, it housed over 1,000 monks committed to day-and-night prayer—intercessory missionaries. They sang hymns and doxologies throughout the night and day. Similar ministries of 24/7 prayer and psalmodic, choral praise were established in other monasteries at that time along the Euphrates and in Persia.

2. *Bangor, Ireland*

In AD 433, Saint Patrick returned to Ireland to preach the gospel. In the twelfth century, the monk Jocelin reported that Patrick had come to a valley on the shores of the Belfast Lough, where he and his comrades beheld a vision of heaven. Jocelin wrote, "They beheld the valley filled with heavenly light, and with a multitude of heaven, they heard, as chanted forth from the voice of angels, the psalmody of the celestial choir." From then on, this place near Bangor was known as the Vale of Angels. Approximately 100 years later, in 558, Comgall established Bangor monastery in that exact valley. Over 3,000 monks joined him in a full-time way. They maintained a 24/7 house of prayer with worship that continued for more than 300 years. Comgall's monastery at Bangor practiced continuous worship that was antiphonal in nature and based on Patrick's vision.

In the twelfth century, Bernard of Clairvaux spoke of Comgall and Bangor, stating that "the solemnization of divine offices was kept up by companies, who relieved each other in succession, so that not for one moment, day or night, was there an intermission of their devotions." These monks, through practicing continual prayer and worship, were stirred to evangelize the lost wherever they went. They were sent out from Bangor as missionaries to Europe. Wherever they settled, they first established constant praise and adoration to God, and their mission work flowed from a foundation of prayer.

These intercessory missionaries were sent to preach the gospel throughout Europe, leading multitudes to Jesus. Examples abound. For instance, Colombanus set out from Bangor with twelve brothers to plant monasteries that combined prayer and mission work throughout Switzerland. Another, Saint Martin, practiced continual antiphonal worship and established monasteries throughout Gaul (France).

3. *Abbot Ambrosius*

Around 522, in Switzerland, Abbot Ambrosius organized choirs of monks who sang the Psalms in rotating shifts, continuing day and night. This continued for nearly 400 years, until around 900, impacting monasteries all over France and Switzerland. These intercessory missionaries were effective in preaching the gospel and impacting many for Jesus.

4. *Cluny, France*

Around 1000, the monastery at Cluny in central France sustained 24/7 prayer with worship because they were convinced that by doing so they were participating in the very worship of heaven, as seen in Revelation 4. Hundreds of monastic communities throughout Europe followed the example of Cluny by embracing 24/7 prayer with worship. Thus the Cluny community was catalytic in raising up intercessory missionaries who established houses of prayer as monastic communities, doing the work of the kingdom.

5. *Bernard of Clairvaux*

Just after 1100, Bernard, together with his 700 monks in Clairvaux, France, organized day-and-night prayer that continued for many years, resulting in a dynamic release of evangelism through signs and wonders across Europe. Bernard promoted continual prayer; reports from visitors to the monastery at Clairvaux speak of the monks singing their prayers through the night and working in silent meditation through the day.

6. *The Moravians and Count Zinzendorf*

In 1727, Count Zinzendorf, a young and wealthy German nobleman, committed his estate in Germany to 24-hour-a-day prayer ministry. About 300 persecuted believers had moved from Bohemia to Zinzendorf's estate, forming a new community named Herrnhut, which means "the watch of the Lord." Zinzendorf gave up his court position to lead this new ministry. They committed to pray in hourly shifts around the clock, all day and night, every day, taking inspiration from Leviticus 6:13, that *the fire must be kept burning; it must not go out.*" This prayer meeting continued non-stop for the next 100 years.

From the prayer room at Herrnhut came a missionary zeal that has hardly been surpassed in Protestant history. By 1776, over 200 missionaries had been sent out from this small community at Herrnhut. These were the first Protestant intercessory missionaries. Zinzendorf became the leader of the first Protestant missionary movement in history. He sent out missionaries, two by two, to unreached people groups. As they were sent out, the prayer furnace back home in Herrnhut covered them. The first Protestant missionary movement married the prayer aspect of evangelism and the Great Commission. Zinzendorf saw prayer and missions as inseparable.

Throughout history we see many examples of an irrefutable principle in God's kingdom: in God's timing, the establishing of night-and-day prayer brings revival in the Church, which leads to significant evangelistic zeal and effectiveness in bringing unbelievers to faith in Jesus. This principle is seen in the fruitful labors of the historical monastic prayer communities that led multitudes of people to Jesus.

7. *The Prayer Movement Today*

The Holy Spirit has raised up thousands of new prayer ministries in the last ten to twenty years. In 1984, the number of 24/7 prayer rooms in the world was fewer than twenty-five. Today, there are over 20,000—and most of that growth has been in the last ten years or so. (Most of these prayer rooms are not led by live worship teams.) New prayer ministries or houses of prayer are springing up all over the globe at a staggering rate. Such momentum in prayer cannot be attributed to human ingenuity but must rather be the sovereign work of the Holy Spirit.

The significant increase of new 24/7 prayer ministries and of large prayer events in stadiums is a prophetic sign of the times, a sign of the approaching day of the Lord's return. In cities around the world, new 24/7 prayer ministries are being established. From Kiev, Bogota, and Jerusalem to New Zealand, Cairo, Cape Town, and Hong Kong, men and women are responding to the Spirit's leadership in this. Despite the pressures and inherent dangers, we see 24/7 prayer centers coming forth in the Muslim world, in nations like Egypt, Turkey, Syria, Indonesia, and Lebanon.

God's desire to be worshiped on earth as He is in heaven has not changed. I believe that some of the principles expressed in the order of worship that God commanded David to embrace are timeless, such as establishing the full-time occupation of singers and musicians in God's house.

However, not everyone is called to be a full-time intercessory missionary. *The greatest ministry is to do the will of God.* In other words, the greatest ministry you can have is the one to which God calls you. If He has called you to serve in the marketplace or in your home, don't despise your calling by trying to imitate the ministry of another. We must embrace our own individual calling because that is the highest calling for each of us.

This call to night-and-day worship and prayer was not emphasized worldwide by the Holy Spirit throughout church history, but He is now calling many ministries to embrace this calling. However, we do not believe that it is God's plan for every local church or ministry to host 24/7 worship and prayer in their own building. We are asking God to establish houses of prayer in each city or region of the earth. This can happen *as many local churches partner together* in the work of night-and-day prayer in their city. The practical application may differ greatly from city to city and from one culture to another.

Many are asking the Lord to establish 24/7 prayer with worship in every tribe and tongue before the Lord returns, by bringing multiple ministries together in unity to accomplish the work in every region of the earth. Imagine a missions movement that reaches every tribe and tongue, preaching the gospel in every language, deeply connected to 24/7 prayer with worship. Will you join me in asking the Lord to establish one million full-time intercessory missionaries before the Lord returns—singers, musicians, sound technicians, intercessors, and gatekeepers maintaining the systems that support these prayer ministries? For some of you, this is your calling, and your personal story is deeply linked to God's plan related to the end-time prayer movement. What a glorious privilege!

10

PRAYER OUTLINES

I. Key Apostolic Prayers and Prophetic Promises

A. Pray for revelation of Jesus' beauty that we might walk in our calling and destiny.

> *17 ... that ... the Father of glory, may give to you the spirit of wisdom and revelation in the knowledge of Him, 18 the eyes of your understanding being enlightened; that you may know [experience] what is the hope of His calling [assurance/clarity of God's call for our life], what are the riches of the glory of His inheritance in the saints [our destiny as Jesus' inheritance], 19 and what is the exceeding greatness of His power toward us who believe, according to the working of His mighty power. (Eph. 1:17–19)*

B. Pray that Jesus' power and presence be manifest in and through us in a greater measure.

> *16 ... that He would grant you, according to the riches of His glory, to be strengthened with might through His Spirit in the inner man, 17 that Christ may dwell [manifest His presence] in your hearts through faith; that you, being rooted and grounded in love, 18 may be able to comprehend [experience] with all the saints what is the width and length and depth and height— 19 to know the love of Christ which passes knowledge; that you may be filled with all the fullness of God. (Eph. 3:16–19)*

C. Pray for God's love to abound in us by the knowledge of God, unto walking in righteousness.

> *9 ... that your love may abound still more and more in knowledge [of God] and all discernment, 10 that you may approve [rejoice in] the things that are excellent, that you may be sincere [no compromise] and without offense till the day of Christ, 11 being filled with the fruits of righteousness. (Phil. 1:9–11)*

D. Pray to know God's will and to be fruitful in ministry and strengthened by intimacy with Him.

> *9 ... that you may be filled with the knowledge of His will in all wisdom and spiritual understanding; 10 that you may walk worthy of the Lord, fully pleasing Him, being fruitful in every good work and increasing in the knowledge of God; 11 strengthened with all might, according to His glorious power, for all patience and longsuffering with joy. (Col. 1:9–11)*

E.   Pray for unity in the Church and to be filled with joy, peace, and hope (confidence).

⁵ May the God of patience and comfort grant you to be like-minded toward one another … ⁶ that you may with one mind and one mouth glorify the … Father … ¹³ may the God of hope fill you with all joy and peace in believing, that you may abound in hope by the power of the Holy Spirit. (Rom. 15:5–6, 13)

F.   Pray to be enriched by all the gifts of the Spirit, including powerful preaching and revelation.

⁵ … that you were enriched in everything by Him in all utterance [anointed preaching] and all knowledge [prophetic revelation], ⁶ even as the testimony of Christ was confirmed in you [by miracles], ⁷ so that you come short in no gift, eagerly waiting for the revelation of … Jesus Christ, ⁸ who will also confirm you to the end, that you may be blameless in the day of our Lord Jesus Christ. (1 Cor. 1:5–8)

G.   Pray for the release of grace to bring the Church to maturity—to abound in love and holiness.

¹⁰ … praying exceedingly that … [God will release His Spirit and grace to] perfect what is lacking in your faith? … ¹² And may the Lord make you increase and abound in love to one another and to all … ¹³ so that He may establish your hearts blameless in holiness before our God and Father at the coming of our Lord Jesus Christ with all His saints. (1 Thes. 3:10–13)

H.   Pray to be worthy (prepared or made spiritually mature) to walk in the fullness of our destiny.

¹¹ … we also pray always for you that our God would count you worthy of [prepare us for] this calling, and fulfill all the good pleasure of His goodness [plans for us] and the work of faith with power, ¹² that the name of … Jesus Christ may be glorified in you, and you in Him, according to the grace of our God … (2 Thes. 1:11–12)

I.   Pray that the Word would increase its influence (effectiveness) as God releases His power.

¹ Pray for us, that the word of the Lord may run swiftly [rapidly increase its influence] and be glorified [confirmed with apostolic power and miracles], just as it is with you … ³ the Lord is faithful, who will establish you and guard you from the evil one … ⁵ may the Lord direct your hearts into the love of God and into the patience [perseverance, or endurance] of Christ. (2 Thes. 3:1–5)

J.   Pray for an impartation of boldness in declaring God's Word with signs and wonders.

29 "Lord … grant to Your servants that with all boldness they may speak Your word, 30 by stretching out Your hand to heal, and that signs and wonders may be done through the name of Your holy Servant Jesus." 31 And when they had prayed, the place where they were assembled together was shaken; and they were all filled with the Holy Spirit, and they spoke the word of God with boldness. (Acts 4:29–31)

K.   Pray for a greater measure of God's power to be released in the midst of His people.

49 "Behold, I send the Promise of My Father upon you; but tarry in the city of Jerusalem until you are endued with power from on high." 50 … He lifted up His hands and blessed them. (Lk. 24:49–50)

L.   Pray for the release of God's promise to pour out His Spirit and release dreams, visions, etc.

17 "'. . . in the last days, says God, that I will pour out of My Spirit on all flesh; your sons and your daughters shall prophesy, your young men shall see visions, your old men shall dream dreams. 18 And on My menservants and on My maidservants I will pour out My Spirit in those days; and they shall prophesy. 19 I will show wonders in heaven above and signs in the earth beneath: blood and fire and vapor of smoke. 20 The sun shall be turned into darkness, and the moon into blood, before the coming of the great and awesome day of the LORD. 21 … whoever calls on the name of the LORD shall be saved.'" (Acts 2:17–21)

M.   Pray for Israel to be saved.

1 My heart's desire and prayer to God for Israel is that they may be saved. (Rom. 10:1)

26 All Israel will be saved … "The Deliverer [Jesus] will come out of Zion, and He will turn away ungodliness from Jacob; 27 for this is My covenant with them, when I take away their sins." (Rom. 11:26–27)

II.   Prayers Based on Song of Solomon [For Use in Worship with the Word Format]

Following are prayers based on key passages from the Song of Solomon, reflecting our journey of growing in love for God. Each one can be used in a Worship with the Word prayer set. (Bold italics indicate words taken from Scripture. Brackets enclose interpretive phrases and/or omissions.)

Prayer based on Song 1:2–4

*(2) **Let him kiss me with the kisses of his mouth** [of Your Word] **for your love is better than wine.** (3) **Because of the fragrance of your good ointments** [Your personality], **your name is ointment poured forth; therefore** [Your people] **love you.** (4) **Draw me** [after You! Let us run together]. **The king has brought me into his chambers. We will be glad and rejoice in you. We will remember your love more than wine. Rightly do** [Your people] **love you.***

Prayer based on Song 1:5–7, 16

*(5) [My heart is dark, but I am lovely to You, O God, even in my weakness!] 7 **O you whom I love,** [come and satisfy my heart.] (16) **Behold, you are** [the beautiful God], **my beloved! Yes,** [so] **pleasant** [to me. I long for you!]*

Prayer based on Song 2:3–5

*(3) **I sat down in his shade** [shade of the cross and Your righteousness] **with great delight, and his fruit was sweet to my taste.** (4) **He brought me to the banqueting** [table], **and his banner** [leadership] **over me was love.** (5) **Sustain me … refresh me with** [more of You], **for I am lovesick.** [You and You alone are my exceedingly great reward.]*

Prayer based on Song 2:8–12

*(8) **The voice of my beloved** [God]! **Behold, he** [conquers] **the mountains** [triumphs over obstacles. (9) He beckons for me to come, leaving my fears behind, trusting in His leadership. (10) I will arise; I will come away with You. (12) The Lord is doing a new thing; the season] **of singing has come,** [the harvest of the nations is at hand].*

Prayer based on Song 2:14, 16; 3:1–4

*(14) [O My Beloved, You long to see our face and to hear our voice; even in our weakness, our voice is sweet, our face is lovely to You.] (16) **My beloved is mine, and I am his.** (3:1) **By night** [I seek] **the one I love.** (2) **"I will seek the one I love"** [until I find Him. (4) When I find Him, I will hold Him and never] **let him go.***

Prayer based on Song 3:11, 4:7–10, 7:10

(11) *[You are King of Kings; we will crown You with our love—the wedding day is coming—]* **the day of the gladness of** *[Your]* **heart.** *[*(4:7)* We are (I am) altogether beautiful to You. *(9)* We (I)]* **have ravished** *[Your heart, we are (I am) Your Bride. *(10)* How beautiful is your love!]* *(7:10)* **I am my beloved's, and his desire is toward me.**

Prayer based on Song 4:16; 5:2

(16) **Awake, O** *[winds of God]*, **blow upon my garden** *[my life, that Your perfumes may flow from me. Beloved God, come near to me. Oh, that my ways would be pleasing to You. *(5:2)* I will open my heart to You; I will not fear; I am Your beloved one.]*

Prayer based on Song 5:8–16; 7:10

(8) *[He is my Beloved;]* **I am lovesick!** *(10)* *[For He is dazzling and excellent in all His ways,]* **chief among ten thousand.** *(11)* **His head** *[leadership]* **is like the finest gold.** *(16)* **His mouth** *[Word]* **is most sweet, yes, he is altogether lovely. This is my beloved, and this is my friend.** *(7:10)* **I am my beloved's, and his desire is toward me.**

Prayer based on Song 8:5–7

(5) **Who is this coming up from the wilderness, leaning upon her beloved?** *(6)* *[I will set You as a seal upon my heart, for Your]* **love is as strong as death** *[comprehensive]*; **its flames are flames of fire.** *(7)* **Many waters** *[temptations/disappointments]* **cannot quench** *[Your]* **love.**

III. Hymns of Revelation [For Use in Worship with the Word Format]

Revelation 1:5–7

⁵ Jesus Christ, the faithful witness ... the ruler over the kings of the earth. To Him who loved us and washed us from our sins in His own blood, ⁶ and has made us kings and priest to His God and Father, to Him be glory and dominion forever and ever. Amen. ⁷ Behold, He is coming with clouds, and every eye will see Him.

Revelation 4:3–8

³ He who sat there was like a jasper and a sardius stone in appearance; and there was a rainbow around the throne, in appearance like an emerald ... ⁵ And from the throne proceeded lightnings, thunderings, and voices [noises, music, choirs] ... ⁶ Before the throne there was a sea of glass, like crystal [mingled with fire] ... ⁸ they do not rest day or night, saying: "Holy, holy, holy, Lord God Almighty, who was and is and is to come!"

Revelation 4:8–11

⁸ They do not rest day or night, saying: "Holy, holy, holy, Lord God Almighty, who was and is and is to come!" ... ¹⁰ the twenty-four elders fall down ... and worship Him ... and cast their crowns before the throne, saying: ¹¹ "You are worthy, O Lord, to receive <u>glory</u> and <u>honor</u> and <u>power</u>; for You created all things, and by Your will [pleasure] they exist and were created."

Revelation 5:9–10

⁹ They sang a new song, saying: "You are worthy to take the scroll, and to open its seals; for You were slain, and have redeemed us to God by Your blood out of every tribe and tongue and people and nation, ¹⁰ and have made us kings and priests to our God; and we shall reign on the earth."

Revelation 5:11–13

¹¹ And I heard the voice of many angels around the throne, [numbering 10,000 times 10,000] ... ¹² saying ... "Worthy is the Lamb who was slain to receive <u>power</u> and <u>riches</u> and <u>wisdom</u>, and <u>strength</u> and <u>honor</u> and <u>glory</u> and <u>blessing</u>!" ¹³ And every creature which is in heaven and on the earth ... I heard saying: "<u>Blessing</u> and <u>honor</u> and <u>glory</u> and <u>power</u> be to Him who sits on the throne, and to the Lamb, forever and ever!"

Revelation 7:9–12

⁹ A great multitude ... of all nations ... ¹⁰ saying, "<u>Salvation</u> belongs to our God ... and to the Lamb!" ¹¹ All the angels ... fell ... before the throne ... ¹² saying: "Amen! <u>Blessing</u> and <u>glory</u> and <u>wisdom</u>, <u>thanksgiving</u> and <u>honor</u> and <u>power</u> and <u>might</u>, be to our God forever and ever. Amen."

Revelation 15:2–4

2 ... a sea of glass mingled with fire, and those who have the victory ... 3 saying: "_Great_ and _marvelous_ are Your works, Lord God Almighty! _Just_ and _true_ are Your ways, O King of the saints! 4 Who shall not _fear_ You, O Lord, and _glorify_ Your name? For You alone are holy. For all nations shall come and worship before You, for Your judgments have been manifested."

Revelation 19:1–7

1 A great multitude in heaven, saying, "Alleluia! _Salvation_ and _glory_ and _honor_ and _power_ belong to the Lord our God! 2 For _true_ and _righteous_ are His judgments" ... 6 "Alleluia! For the Lord God omnipotent reigns! 7 Let us be _glad_ and _rejoice_ and give Him _glory_, for the marriage of the Lamb has come, and His wife has made herself ready."

Revelation 19:11–16

11 He ... was called Faithful and True, and in righteousness He judges and makes war. 12 His eyes were like a flame of fire, and on His head were many crowns ... 13 His name is called The Word of God. 14 And the armies in heaven ... followed Him ... 15 out of His mouth goes a sharp sword, that with it He should strike the nations ... He Himself treads the winepress of the _fierceness and wrath of Almighty God_. 16 And He has ... a name written: KING OF KINGS AND LORD OF LORDS.

Revelation 22:16–17

16 "I, Jesus ... the Bright and Morning Star." 17 The Spirit and the bride say, "Come!"

International House *of* Prayer
MISSIONS BASE OF KANSAS CITY

....

24/7 Live Worship with Prayer since 1999

On September 19, 1999, a prayer meeting began that continues to this day; from dawn to dusk and through the watches of the night, by the grace of God, prayer and worship have continued twenty-four hours a day, seven days a week.

Learn more at ihopkc.org/about

THE PRAYER ROOM EXPERIENCE

Unceasing is a monthly subscription to our exclusive, growing library of spontaneous worship recorded live at the International House of Prayer. Every month we add our best songs, prophetic moments, intercession cycles, and instrumental selahs.

Learn more at unceasingworship.com

International House of Prayer Missions Base, 3535 E. Red Bridge Road, Kansas City, MO 64137
(816) 763-0200 | info@ihopkc.org

INTERNATIONAL
HOUSE *of* PRAYER
UNIVERSITY

MINISTRY • MUSIC • MEDIA • MISSIONS

· ·

ENCOUNTER GOD. DO HIS WORKS. CHANGE THE WORLD.

ihopkc.org/ihopu

· ·

International House of Prayer University (IHOPU) is a full-time Bible school which exists to equip this generation in the Word and in the power of the Holy Spirit for the bold proclamation of the Lord Jesus and His return.

As part of the International House of Prayer, our Bible school is built around the centrality of the Word and 24/7 prayer with worship, equipping students in the Word and the power of the Spirit for the bold proclamation of the Lord Jesus and His kingdom. Training at IHOPU forms not only minds but also lifestyle and character, to sustain students for a life of obedience, humility, and anointed service in the kingdom. Our curriculum combines in-depth biblical training with discipleship, practical service, outreach, and works of compassion.

IHOPU is for students who long to encounter Jesus. With schools of ministry, music, media, and missions, our one- to four-year certificate and diploma programs prepare students to engage in the Great Commission and obey Jesus' commandments to love God and people.

"What Bible School has 'prayer' on its curriculum? The most important thing a man can study is the prayer part of the Book. But where is this taught?

Let us strip off the last bandage and declare that many of our presidents and teachers do not pray, shed no tears, know no travail. Can they teach what they do not know?"

–Leonard Ravenhill, *Why Revival Tarries*

International House of Prayer University, 12901 S. US Highway 71, Grandview, MO 64030
(816) 763-0243 | info@ihopu.org

International House *of* Prayer
INTERNSHIPS

INTRO TO IHOPKC • FIRE IN THE NIGHT • ONE THING INTERNSHIP
SIMEON COMPANY • HOPE CITY INTERNSHIP

ihopkc.org/internships

Internships exist to see people equipped with the Word of God, ministering in the power of the Holy Spirit, engaged in intercession, and committed to outreach and service.

Our five internships are three to six months long and accommodate all seasons of life. The purpose of the internships is to further prepare individuals of all ages as intercessors, worshipers, messengers, singers, and musicians for the work of the kingdom. While each internship has a distinctive age limit, length, and schedule, they all share the same central training components: corporate prayer and worship meetings, classroom instruction, practical ministry experience, outreach, and relationship-building.

Biblical teaching in all of the internships focuses on intimacy with Jesus, ministry in the power of the Holy Spirit, the forerunner ministry, evangelizing the lost, justice, and outreach. Interns also receive practical, hands-on training in the prophetic and healing ministries.

Upon successful completion of a six-month internship or two three-month tracks, some will stay and apply to join IHOPKC staff.

Our IHOPKC Leadership Team

Our leadership team of over a hundred and fifty men and women, with diversity of experience, background, and training, represent twenty countries and thirty denominations and oversee eighty-five departments on our missions base. With a breadth of experience in pastoral ministry, missions work, education, and the marketplace, this team's training in various disciplines includes over forty master's degrees and ten doctorates.

International House of Prayer Missions Base, 3535 E. Red Bridge Road, Kansas City, MO 64137
(816) 763-0200 | internships@ihopkc.org

MIKE BICKLE
TEACHING LIBRARY
—— *Free Teaching & Resource Library* ——

This International House of Prayer resource library, encompassing more than thirty years of Mike's teaching ministry, provides access to hundreds of resources in various formats, including streaming video, downloadable video, and audio, accompanied by study notes and transcripts, absolutely free of charge.

You will find some of Mike's most requested titles, including *The Gospel of Grace*; *The First Commandment*; *Jesus, Our Magnificent Obsession*; *Romans: Theology of Holy Passion*; *The Sermon on the Mount: The Kingdom Lifestyle*; and much more.

We encourage you to freely copy any of these teachings to share with others or use in any way: "our copyright is the right to copy." Older messages are being prepared and uploaded from Mike's teaching archives, and all new teachings are added immediately.

Visit mikebickle.org

International House of Prayer Missions Base, 3535 E. Red Bridge Road, Kansas City, MO 64137
(816) 763-0200 | info@ihopkc.org | ihopkc.org